SWIMMING CHICKENS

SWIMMING CHICKENS

and Other Half-Breasted Accounts of the Animal World

Colin McEnroe

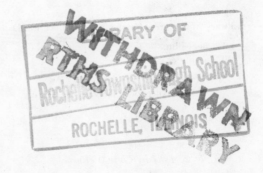

A DOLPHIN BOOK
Doubleday
New York
1987

Some of the material in this book appeared previously in the Hartford *Courant* and is used here under license granted by the Hartford Courant Co.

26212

Library of Congress Cataloging-in-Publication Data

McEnroe, Colin.
  Swimming chickens.

  "A Dolphin book."
  1. Animals—Anecdotes, facetiae, etc. I. Title.
QL791.M356 1987   818'.5403   87-553
ISBN 0-385-23993-9

Dedicated to my grandmother, Alma Cotton, who was a pioneer in pigeon birth control and who always saw the comical magic in animals and who once, when I was little, impersonated a dinosaur so successfully that I was obliged to shoot her in the forehead with a rubber-tipped dart.

Sorry about that, Grandma, but I really thought you were a dinosaur.

Acknowledgments

I mainly regard this book as a Nietzschean triumph of my individual will, so if you are looking for your name in here, you may be in for one of life's little disappointments.

But it would probably be a good idea to mention my sweet wife, Thona, who puts up with a lot. And my mother and my father. My father once drove me all the way down to the Bronx Zoo so I could see the Komodo dragon there, and when we arrived, they didn't have it. It was not clear what they had done with it. Sent it out to be dry-cleaned, maybe. And my mother once had a pet turkey which she walked on a leash.

And then there's Roy Blount, Jr. He not only inspired me, he also introduced me to Esther Newberg, the most powerful woman in publishing. Or Western culture in general, for that matter. Thanks to Roy and Esther and Jim Fitzgerald, who said it would be fine if I didn't write anything about dolphins. Dolphins make me nervous. I like them, mind you. But how much do they really know?

And thanks to my generously talented colleagues at the Hartford *Courant* and to the *Courant* itself, made flesh in Mike Davies, for letting me use some material which formed the basis for much of this book.

Okay, so maybe you are in here, after all.

Contents

Bitter Pills

Now and then, I am called upon to give my dog a pill.

Here is what happens. I open the dog's mouth. I shove the pill back as far as it will go. I close the dog's mouth. I wait a decent interval. I release the dog's snout. Life goes on.

The dog looks at me gratefully, as if to say, "What was that? It was for my own good, wasn't it? Yessir, you wouldn't do it if it weren't. I appreciate your taking the time."

Leaves me feeling like James Herriot, this does.

I am always a little astonished at the ease of the operation because I grew up with cats, who harbor an entirely different attitude toward pill-taking. A cat regards the administering of medicine as a situation in which it may fling aside whatever social constraints it has adopted over the years and try, fang and claw, to destroy you.

"I may be sick unto death," the cat says, "but if I go, I'm taking you with me."

Forget about sneaking the pill into the cat's food. You could serve the cat an entire ground ox with a tiny minced pill stirred in, and when you returned to your kitchen later, the ox would be gone. Strewn across the floor, however, there would be particles which, if assembled, would constitute one perfect streptomycin tablet.

Forget about gratitude too. Most cats, like Mildred in *Of Human*

Bondage, accept hovering attentions with a kind of vaguely understood resentment. You could drive your dogsled across the frozen tundra for four sleepless days and nights, pick up the penicillin in Nome, drive your dogsled back, and the cat would use the last full measure of its ebbing life force to open up your leg—down to the shinbone.

As a boy, I had a cat named Mackenzie who was particularly adamant in his opposition to pills. I can remember one terribly worrisome night when my father and I tried to administer medication to him. I don't know how I succeeded in involving my father in the project. He didn't like cats and, when we had them, always insisted on not knowing their names. He addressed them and referred to them by their colors: "Hello, brown cat," or "I saw the gray-and-white cat devouring a toad near the driveway."

I also don't remember what was wrong with Mackenzie. It was not a syndrome which produced lethargy. Mackenzie scored heavily on us in the early rounds. Any decent ref would have stopped the fight.

From time to time, Mackenzie would make a noise worthy of Linda Blair and the pill would fly from our midst and skitter across the floor into a dark corner.

In desperation, we called our vet, but he was out. His calls were being handled by another vet, who was, unfortunately, out of his mind. "Wrap kitty up in a blanket so that just kitty's little head is sticking out," he said in a prissy voice. We began to wonder if we had, by some twist of telecommunications, reached Jonathan Winters by mistake.

Once we had kitty bundled up thusly, we should open his little mouth and toss the pill down his little throat, advised the vet.

We decided to try it. My father and I wrapped Mackenzie tighter than Tut (during which process we lost only about a cup and a half of blood between us—quite cheap by Mackenzian standards). As we tried to get the pill into his mouth, Mackenzie began to writhe in a manner disturbingly reminiscent of Houdini.

"I think one of kitty's little paws is about to get loose," I told my father, just as said paw appeared out of one of the folds and began swiping around like a scorpion's tail.

There are two things you can do in a situation like that. One is to move briskly and decisively, while you still hold a putative advantage, to secure the loose paw and then complete the job as efficiently as possible. The second thing is to decide immediately that you are going to throw the whole kit and caboodle in one direction and then run like a son of a gun in the other.

My father and I did neither. Tapes analyzed subsequently by the Nuclear Regulatory Commission revealed that we fumbled equivocally for a few critical seconds until, somehow, the total Mackenzie had emerged, with a full arsenal of sharp points. My father and I will be forgiven for believing that the antichrist had arrived on earth. His vengeance was terrible and swift.

The following day, my father and I trudged into the vet's office carrying a basket which we had covered with a sheet of plywood. We wore thick gauntlets on our hands and hollow stares on our faces. The basket emitted a low, guttural sound which was not of this earth.

"What . . . what have you got in there?" asked the vet, with the air of a man who wonders if he is licensed (or even inclined) to treat Tasmanian devils.

"A cat," said my father and I, with the air of men who have returned from the front after seeing horrors to which no words can possibly do justice.

I honestly don't remember what the vet decided to do. It seems possible that he decided my father and I needed pills a lot more than the cat did at that point.

Many years have passed. My father has recovered nearly the full use of his arms.

So it was with great interest that I read, a while back, about Harold Farkley, a Midwestern man who is (or was) suing a defunct restaurant because a stray cat attacked him twice. Actually, Harold Farkley was not his name, but, feeling that he and his wife have suffered enough, I have voluntarily altered their monikers.

According to the maddeningly incomplete wire-service news item I read, Farkley claimed he was permanently scarred and traumatized by the cat "who bit and scratched him on two hot summer nights." Farkley complained that the cat fed on garbage from the restaurant and that the restaurant staff did not restrain the cat after the first attack.

Most fascinating of all, Lydia Farkley, Harold's wife, filed a suit of her own because "the marriage hasn't been the same since her husband was injured."

The news item did not make it clear precisely whom Lydia was suing.

Perhaps, in this litigious world, she found it necessary to sue her husband, the restaurant, and the cat (just in case some little old lady has willed the cat a massive fortune, giving the cat, as barristers are wont to say, "deep pockets").

I have felt a great need to discuss this case with someone, but I don't know whom to call. The restaurant, as we have said, is defunct, and the cat is presumably on the lam. It seems wrong to intrude upon the private hell of the Farkleys.

I imagine they sit in silence, most evenings.

Occasionally, unable to stand it one minute longer, Harold Farkley will hurl his newspaper to the floor and shout, "It was an especially large cat!"

"Yes dear, I know," Lydia will murmur. "We've already been through that and—"

"If people could have been there, *seen* the monster . . ."

Wait. Perhaps I have it wrong. Perhaps Harold is reading not a newspaper but a book—*Using Tae Kwan Do to Subdue Small and Medium-Sized Animals.* He has been practicing in the basement and is itching to have another go at that cat. He is tired of being known as the guy who is 0–2 against a tabby.

What with the restaurant being defunct, he cannot find his nemesis. He hangs around on street corners late at night with a mackerel hanging out of his coat pocket. (Small wonder Lydia feels their union has lost a certain something.) He taunts other cats, but they slink away.

Actually, it is hard to imagine a cat picking a fight. Surely the restaurant staff would not have allowed the cat to live off their garbage if the cat habitually attacked customers. Farkley must, then, have been a unique case. The cat did not like the cut of his jib.

The nearest thing to an unprovoked cat attack I have ever seen involved a cat who accosted me once in New Haven. It was a stormy day, and I wore a trench coat. The cat cocked its head at me in a peculiar way, raced over, and climbed the length of my trench coat and, by extension, me. Ascending to my shoulders, it put its paws on my head, had a look around, and jumped down.

I was unscathed, but I worried that I looked compromised and foolish. I was a college student at the time, and I generally looked quite foolish and compromised enough, thank you, without any help from cats using me as their personal Matterhorn.

Unlike Farkley, I was not married, and I cannot even guess how it would have affected my nuptial bond. I did not see fit to include the incident when I listed my shortcomings to my wife-to-be years later.

Anyway, I know a little of what Harold Farkley may feel.

I am disturbed, nonetheless, by the idea that the Farkley marriage is not the same since the attacks.

Everything hinges, of course, on what the marriage was like before the attacks. It is possible, on the one hand, that in winning the hand of the fair Lydia, Harold represented himself as someone who could give cats what for. (In legal circles, this is the esteemed doctrine of *quoquo vincet felinum.*) Now that illusion lies in tatters, and soon the hot summer nights will be returning on little, um, mouse feet.

On the other hand lies the possibility that there is (and always has been) something oddly catlike about Lydia and that Harold now recoils in her presence. (I don't know what the hell this is called in legal circles.) It is even possible, although only remotely, that Lydia was in the habit of lounging around the house in a cat costume, in somewhat happier times.

There is a good deal to be said about the curious triangle of men, women, and cats, and I hope to say some of it in a later chapter of this book, if my strength holds out. But expecting American jurisprudence to unravel this mess is asking a lot. As Oliver Wendell Holmes, Jr., once said, "No law has been written yet that can anticipate the actions of cats."

Well, no, actually, he never said that, but that's the sort of thing he tended to say.

If I were the judge in this case, I believe I would urge the Farkleys to look into their hearts and find strength. I might share with them some of my pharmacopoeial war stories. True love and matrimony have become devalued commodities indeed if they cannot survive two cat assaults, I would conclude.

And if it was a hot summer night, I believe I would ask the bailiff to walk me out to my car.

No More Bad Bugs

There was one on the windshield this morning, and he clung there for the entire drive into work.

A bug. He lay spread-eagled (or spread-bugged) across my windshield, right in my line of sight. Leering at me. For miles. He was green and yellow with a red head, and slanted wings, like an F-111. Probably an experimental bug, escaped from some government lab.

It's the spring rains, you see. Try to find someone to take responsibility for polychromatic mutant bugs on your automobile and what you will hear is a bunch of lame mutterings about the spring rains.

Entomologists have apparently discovered that every third spring raindrop hits the ground and promptly divides into four earwigs, twelve mosquitoes, one cricket, two houseflies, seven beetles, one radioactive redyellowgreen windshield-clinging Exocet spittlebug, and enough nutrient-enriched filth to nurse them all into robust adulthood.

You may remember reading, as a child, in the *Golden Wonder Book of the Living World of Exciting and Fun Bugs*, about the thrilling panoply of roughly 9 jillion species of insect, each as marvelously different from one another as snowflakes.

Don't believe it.

Bugs would like nothing better than for us humans to waste

enormous bundles of time classifying them. A much more useful way of understanding bugs involves breaking them down into four easy-to-remember categories.

1. Bugus horrificus: bugs with massive, serrated, flesh-tearing jaws

2. Bugus terribilis: bugs with massive, hooked, flesh-puncturing stingers full of disease-causing venom

3. Bugus disgustibus: bugs which exude toxic, germ-infested, nauseating rabid purple slime

4. Bugus invisibilis: bugs so tiny you can't see them at all but which can bite the bejabbers out of you

That's it. Anyone tells you there are other kinds of bugs, chances are he's on their payroll. Look into it.

The reason I know so much about bugs is that my yard is kind of a bug tourist mecca. Many is the time I have confiscated from a captured bug (usually wearing a brightly colored shirt) a tiny, shiny brochure advertising "Club McEnroe!—Acres of Delightfully Brackish Foul-Smelling Water. Feast on Crumbs, Blood, and Human Epidermis in Our Dining Rooms. Dance the Night Away in Our Outer-Ear Lounge While Our Invisible Orchestra Plays All Your Favorite High-Pitched Insectoid Whines!"

These annoyances notwithstanding, I make it my policy not to kill bugs.

There was a wasp nest on the side of our garage for weeks, and I was all for not doing anything about it. I take the cosmic view, which is that wasps—by the way, I use the terms "wasp" and "hornet" pretty much interchangeably because, frankly, I don't know the difference—have just as much right to a little niche in the universe as I do.

Anyway, I'm all for not doing anything about most situations.

I did not take the cosmic view the previous summer when we had strange, mutant *Hellstrom Chronicle* wasps who made an audible munching noise as they ate the unwholesome chemical varnish off the fake wood armrests of our stylish lawn chairs.

I didn't do anything about them either, but it was only because I couldn't think of anything to do.

They didn't lend themselves to traditional anti-bug weapons

and tactics. I don't believe they had a nest or that they e\
that matter, slept. Mostly they just ate armrests. Eventually, \
took in so many unstable chemicals that they simply vanished int\
another dimension.

Still, you cannot expect many of life's problems to work themselves out so neatly for you.

And let's give wasps their due. They are peculiarly stalwart
animals. My old college roommate, Kenneth V. B. Jennings of
Landover, Maryland, liked to tell of a wasp he attempted to kill by
flinging handfuls of gravel down upon it, like an Old Testament
judgment. Bloodied (or gooied, anyway) but unbowed, the wasp
kept dragging itself up off the canvas and tottering its gravel-drunk
body around. I forget how it came out. You had to hear Kenneth
V. B. Jennings tell it, with all the rawboned grit of a Robert Service poem (except I don't believe Robert Service ever referred to
anyone as "that sucker").

Yet, for all their indomitability, wasps also have an unmistakably careworn mien (if the insect world admits of miens). In repose
(if wasps can be said to repose), wasps often look scrunched and
fretful, like stockbrokers in the midst of an especially bearish
downturn.

Where was I? Ah, the nest. I was all for letting the nest be. Just
on the off chance that this new family of wasps might up and
follow its forebears into the eighth dimension.

And then small boys discovered it.

Believe you me, no class of persons ranges so far afield from the
cosmic perspective as do small boys. No class of persons embraces
so wholeheartedly the first-strike doctrine of let's do it to them just
in case somewhere down the line it might enter their heads to do
something to us.

I know whereof I write. As a small boy, I was drawn into numerous sorties against prospering colonies of stinging insects, usually under the generalship of a boy named Crawford Brash.

Crawford's Waterloo was a colony of yellow jackets living in a
hole under the sidewalk. He just couldn't bear to leave it alone and
eventually worked out an Entebbe-style raid in which squirt-gun-

ould lay down cover fire while a demolitions team dropped
ackers down the hole.

My memory of Crawford's exact role in this sally is disturbingly
hazy, but he badly underestimated the Divine Wind of yellow
jacket flying aces who swooped down and routed the whole operation. We of the 23rd Squirt Gun Artillery held our positions for a
gritty four seconds or so and then fled.

I went home stung. Few tears were shed in my household for
sting victims. My mother often yelled at me for getting stung. This
has something to do—in a very unfair way—with the fact that in
the early days of their marriage, she reached my father at work
with a shrieking, incoherent phone call about a medical emergency. He rushed home to find that she had been stung by a bee.

Anyway, my mind was a tumult of these ragged memories and
unsettled scores one day when I came home and discovered a knot
of small boys milling near the above-mentioned wasp nest.

The nest was a gaping wound, ripped asunder by a missile.
Pieces of dangling gray wasp paper looped, beardlike, below what
was left of the nest, causing the whole affair to look like someone's
unsuccessful attempt to make an origami of Walt Whitman's head.

"Did you know about the wasps?" a helpful small boy asked me.

"Yes. And don't throw rocks at them because . . ." Because
why? Here I groped for the proper deterrent language. Something
with an unmistakable quality of menace while avoiding those
you'll-shrivel-up-and-die clichés. Small boys see through those
with the clairvoyance of Jedi masters. ". . . because you could get
real sick if they stung you." Okay, so I'm a little lame on imagery.

"They already did sting us," one small boy said flatly.

"My neighbor died last night. We're going to go look at the body
at seven-thirty," another small boy informed me soberly, without,
as far as I could see, tying it in to the situation at hand.

"Good God," I told him.

The small boys looked at me and I at them. I tried to think of
something cosmic to say but found myself at a loss for words. It
struck me that I should spend more time talking to small boys,
who, for all their garishness, live very close to the pith and marrow

of life. They remind me of those priests of animism in Togo who believe that spirits and demons dwell in all things.

I went back to check on the wasps, who were in a Damage Control mode. They looked even more played out than usual. Clearly didn't have a piece of the rock for their nest.

Wasps and the cosmos aside, there are several other good reasons why I do not kill bugs.

1. I have no idea, in general, what goes on in the afterlife. It may be a bugiarchy, in which bugs are the dominant spiritual order and exact vengeance on anyone who messed with them in life.

Just in case that's true, I occasionally propitiate the bugs in this world. Maybe throw a pork chop out into the backyard at night and listen to the piranhalike sounds of gnashing, slobbering bug pincers. About thirty seconds later, the dry, stripped bone flies back out of the blackness and clatters onto the porch.

2. Bugs eat other bugs. This is a known fact. You kill one bug and you simply make it possible for a smaller, creepier class of bug to prosper.

At the heart of this vaguely Marxist bugview (in the original German, *Volkswagenschauung*) is the spider. I try to manipulate the class struggle by making my house a spider refuge and pumping steroids into the little guys. My feeling is that one or two bloated industrialist spider barons who are more or less in my pocket would be preferable to several hundred small free-lance insects.

Unfortunately, the spiders' idea of gratitude to me is to crawl into my bed at night and lacerate my face.

3. Conventional anti-bug weaponry is useless.

There is no record of one single bug dying from a household bug spray. Most sprays will cause a bug to lie quietly for about forty-five seconds, after which the bug will spring up feeling renewed, refreshed, chemically mutated, and therefore able to fly at supersonic speeds and inject previously unknown poisons into the person who sprayed it.

Anyway, if you read the fine print on the labels, the manufacturers of these nostrums pretty much throw up their hands over the issue of whether their toxins are more dangerous to insects or to humans.

Forget about electric zappers too. Bugs are much too smart to fly into them and mostly use them to execute mutinous bugs who refuse to subscribe to anti-people policies.

My neighbor installed one of those zappers, and—despite the fact that our neighborhood looks like open auditions for insect extras in an Indiana Jones movie—the thing goes "nyaaaawk" about once every seventeen minutes. Just often enough to make me queasily aware that charred insect parts are drifting on the night breeze outside my window.

So, until I heard about John G. Hildebrand, I pretty much let the bugs have their way. Every night, they somehow arrive in my kitchen and begin circling around and around the overhead light like the motorcycle gang in *The Wild One.* I have no idea what they want. Possibly they have no idea either. It's just something to do.

In the pre-Hildebrandean universe, I had two options:

• Say, "There go those insects again, Estelle." I reject that option because it is lame, because I should have something snappier to say to bugs, and because I don't know anyone named Estelle.

• Snap a dish towel at them. I reject that option too, because I would kill maybe one or two insects every hour and almost certainly cause the overhead light cover to crash to the floor and imbed shards of glass in my flesh, setting off a feeding frenzy among all the blood-gargling insects who ordinarily wait patiently for me to go to bed before they start grazing on me.

Along cometh John G. Hildebrand, a University of Arizona neurobiologist who believes, according to a news article I read, that the future of insect control lies in behavior modification.

He has not, far as I know, taught any flea beetles to fetch his pipe and slippers, but that will come. We're here at the dawning of Hildebrandean thought.

A lonely voice crying in the Arizona desert, Hildebrand says teach your insects well. Look at each insect as a behavior problem. Insect Town. "There are no bad insects." That kind of thing.

We Hildebrandeans believe you got to mess with the insect's mind. Get him so hooked on what you want him to do that he doesn't even remember his old ways. Kind of surprising that no one has come forward with this idea before now. I mean, we are, after all, smarter than insects, aren't we? Well, aren't we? Awright, let's hear a little spirit out there.

One of Hildebrand's sample ideas concerns mosquitoes: Get mosquitoes on the wagon. Get them off the milk of human blood. Hildebrand would manipulate their behavior so that they only drink rabbit blood or squirrel blood. Doesn't go far enough, in my view. It remains for us disciples who come after the prophet to interpret and expand his teachings. Let's go whole hog and persuade the mosquitoes to suck on zucchinis and fruitcake, thus ridding the common weal of two bothersome surpluses.

With that example in mind, let us look at a few other bothersome insects from a Hildebrandean vantage:

• Beetles. I mean the great big black ones. What do you want them to do? Stop clinging to your screen door at night, right? You open the inside door and waaaugh! there are bunches of them crimped on there, humming and nattering. So we need to redirect their clinging impulses. Get 'em to cling to such itinerant salespersons, mountebanks, etc., as set foot on our property.

"What's, ugh, what's that?"

"Oh, he's just playing. No, don't run from him. He thinks that's part of the game."

• Moths. Want 'em to calm down and stop eating our vestments, don't we? How hard is that? First we work on the aimless, irksome fluttering. Smooth out their karmas, do some biofeedback, get them to be less Type A. Then put them on a strict diet of dog hair. (I offer it by the truckload in the summer.) Let them binge, maybe once a week, by swarming down on a fluorescently garbed golfer. This worked for Liz Taylor. (The bingeing part, I mean.)

• Slugs. As Hildebrandeans, we need to get past our disgust at slugs and see what they could be in an entomological Walden Two. Yes, slugs are fat, slimy, indolent garden destroyers. But they don't have to be. Teach them self-respect. Encourage them to get a little sun, eat less, move around more. Give them a project. Anything. It can be a real New Deal type of job. Tell thirty of them they have four hours to move a lawn chair across the patio. Sure, they probably won't make it, but the fact that you believed in them will count for a lot. Reward them like crazy if they make it even halfway. In no time at all, you'll have lean, tan, muscular slugs with Erno Laszlo complexions and helpful attitudes.

• Gnats. I wouldn't say Hildebrandean thought breaks down over gnats, but it comes up a little short. You want gnats to stop flying around you and yours, going up noses, etc. That, really, is all gnats do, and it may be asking too much to expect them to develop a whole new career.

So maybe there's a bit of a snag with the gnats, but there is little doubt that Hildebrandean thinking is really going to take off, once we get the bugs out.

Hmmmm? . . . Sorry, I have to go. They want another pork chop.

Poules Rush In

There was no chance that any of us would get through this book without a chapter on chickens.

If all the humorists in history could be polled on the matter of what animal is inherently the funniest, chickens would win going away. We would be held just short of unanimity by a few home-town favorites such as tapirs and slow lorises.

For all that, I don't believe anyone has ever gotten at what is so funny about a chicken, and rest assured that this mean scrivener is not even going to try. I intend only to call your attention to a few recent developments out there on the farthest-flung frontiers of chickendom.

The first of these items appeared several years ago as a wire-service story buried inside the Boston *Globe*. It was based on a report from Tass, the Soviet news agency, and if it was true, the *Globe* had a hell of a nerve putting it anywhere but on page one.

"Soviet scientists have bred amphibious chickens which fearlessly leap into pools and spend hours pecking grain underwater," the article began. Similar experiments had been carried out on mice, rabbits, monkeys, cats, and, in the article's words, "their offspring," a phrase which hoists up warning flags in the mind. Wouldn't the offspring of mice be mice? Unless they are interbreeding the above-mentioned species, a fearsome prospect indeed.

An amphibious chicken is a pleasantly bracing thought. An amphibious monkeyrabbit is a sticking point at summit talks.

The article went on to quote Soviet scientist Igor Charkovski as saying, "After the full training course, the offspring not only swam and dived freely but even ate, slept and, in a word, lived underwater."

And there the article ended.

I hate it when that happens. You're just starting to get interested, maybe a little frightened, by the whole idea. Mmmmmmm, amphibious chickens. Do we have any? Is there an amphibious chicken gap? But there is nothing more to read. If the *Globe* is going to raise the specter of swimming chickens, the *Globe* ought to feel some obligation to pursue the whole story. I suppose no editor wanted to go into the afternoon news conference and say, "I think we ought to hit this amphibious chicken story real hard." So they wound up running this half-breasted account.

You also have to ask yourself why a satanic empire would be leaking out this kind of information. It smacks of a hoax, intended to make us so obsessed with the chicken gap that our attention is diverted from more practical sorts of ordnance.

The only way I, as an artist, could respond to the subject was to create something. Thus, I have written a play about Igor Charkovski. Or possibly an opera or motion picture, I'm not sure. Feel free to assign parts to your loved ones and neighbors and perform it in the parlor on winter evenings. You needn't send me royalties. I intend it only as a parable.

20,000 LEGHORNS UNDER THE SEA: A GEOPOLITICAL DRAMA IN ONE ACT

(Author's note: I sorely regret the absence of any mention of pigs in the report on the Soviet experiment because I really wanted to call this *Porky Park*, but I will not abuse my artistic license so extravagantly as to insert pigs where they have no business being.)

Cast:

Dr. Igor Charkovski, a high-principled Soviet aqua-vivisectionist

Sonya, a chicken
Vladimir Perdusky of the KGB
A wombat

We open on Dr. Charkovski standing at the side of a long swimming pool. He holds a stopwatch.

CHARKOVSKI: (shouts) Go! (Sonya, his most cherished amphibious chicken, plunges in and swims the length of the pool underwater.) Twelve point six seconds! (Charkovski towels off the wet chicken.) Oh, Sonya, you have surpassed your best mark.

SONYA: (business).

Enter Perdusky, unseen.

PERDUSKY: Very good, Comrade Igor.

CHARKOVSKI: You! I thought I told you to stay out of my lab.

PERDUSKY: We must talk.

CHARKOVSKI: Not now, I have a wombat in the Jacuzzi. He's due to surface any second.

PERDUSKY: Your foolish academic games have been useful to us, but that usefulness is at an end. It is time to commence Operation Chicken o' the Sea. Thousands of your chickens will be released from submarines off the coast of Cape Cod. They will make their way ashore by night, with blackened faces.

CHARKOVSKI: Surely even you would not use them to destabilize the Americanski chicken population . . .

PERDUSKY: You are exactly precise. They will entice other chickens into lakes, rivers, swimming pools. The capitalist chickens will drown. By that time, the monkeyrabbits we will have released in the Great Lakes—

CHARKOVSKI: (a horrified scream) No! Not the monkeyrabbits!

PERDUSKY: Yes. Ha, the Americanski pawns. While they have squandered precious time trying to breed communist pandas, we have taken the common chicken and made it a tool of power, a Nietzschean superfowl! And *she* will lead them all. (Snatches Sonya from Charkovski's arms.)

SONYA: (ad lib).

CHARKOVSKI: No, please! Do what you will, but do not take my beloved Sonya.

PERDUSKY: Sentimental fool! (Shoves Charkovski into swimming pool. Rushes to door at stage right.)

CHARKOVSKI: No! Not that door!

Perdusky, harking too late, if at all, has stepped through door and plunged into the Jacuzzi. The frenzied wombat attacks him and blood rises to the water's frothing surface. Charkovski flounders clumsily to the pool's edge and climbs out and rushes through the door to find Sonya perched on the Jacuzzi's rim.

CHARKOVSKI: Come, little one.

Tucking Sonya under his arm, he runs into the cold Smolensk night, with only his hope for a saner world to guide him to refuge.

CURTAIN

I'm not wedded to the title, actually. I haven't ruled out something like *Rhode Island Red Dawn* or *As Those Capons Go Rolling Along.* The money, obviously, would be in future spin-offs: *Night of the Living Monkeyrabbits, Part XXVLMI*, that sort of thing.

Do not imagine, however, that mad poultry science is a stranger to our own shores. Not so. Consider Dr. Joseph Vandepopuliere (a name I would have given a lot to have made up), an American scientist who has dared to tinker with the egg itself.

Even if his audacious egg experiments never work out, the name of "Dr. Joe," as he is apparently known, Vandepopuliere is already written large (but not too large, else it would not fit) on the escutcheon of science.

He has already invented the "extruded" (cooked, puffed, and processed) dog, cat, trout, and monkey chows so many of us feed our dogs, cats, trout, and monkeys. And he has also invented—I swear this is true—the chicken brassiere.

Yes. Vandepopuliere, a professor of poultry science at the University of Missouri–Columbia, holds a patent on a little padded brassiere which one puts on future broiler chickens in order to prevent them from damaging the breast meat while cavorting in this life. Other people, of course, use them for religious purposes.

It just goes to show you that it's the doers in this life who reap the laurels, not to mention the big mazuma. The fact is, I myself have thought of chicken brassieres. Or at least, I have thought of chickens *in* brassieres. Not for any reason, really. I have just thought of them. From time to time.

The only thing standing between me and the greatness now enjoyed by Dr. Joe was a short walk down to the patent office. Plus finding out where the patent office is located. I imagine it might also be hard to get the clerk there to take one seriously. About chicken brassieres. I am not one to subject myself to a lot of "I Dreamed I Stomped Wade Boggs to Death Last Night in My McEnroe Bra" jokes.

Anyway, if you think Dr. Joe is resting on his chicken brassieres (and that is absolutely the last time I am going to mention them), you misjudge the Vandepopuliere mettle. He has turned his keen mind to the subject of eggs and has asked the question from which lesser men have shrunk: Why should eggs have shells?

It has occurred to Dr. Joe that chickens put a good deal of time and biochemical effort into making eggshells, which don't get used by anybody except the Easter Bunny and people who teach their grandmothers to suck eggs. If chickens could be persuaded to ease up on the shells, they would be able to devote more inner chicken wherewithal to producing the eggs—or thus sprach Vandepopuliere. Chickens would lay more eggs, which would be good for agribusiness, which would be good for America. Excelsior!

Actually, "Excelsior" might be a bad thing to say to a chicken, whose entire livelihood depends on downward progress (unless Vandepopuliere intends to have eggs emerge from some other opening).

I made bold to telephone Vandepopuliere after reading about him. One of the many things I am nonetheless hazy about is the pronunciation of his name. I tend to give it a ta-ra-ra-BOOM-de-ay cadence. Thus we sing:

VandepoPOOliere
What is so wondrous fair
As a fine egg that's bare
Of any outer layer?

I wanted to ask Dr. Joe how, exactly, he intended to alter chickens so radically. Build a better chicken and the world will beat an

egg to your door. But I am a stranger to the art of chicken manipu-
lation—to me, a chicken's body is a temple—so I couldn't imagine
where one would begin.

Dr. Joe said the job is still in the embryonic stages—ha!—but it
would probably involve a combination of feeding, lighting, and
finagling at the genetic level. (I imagine that, at first, the chickens
will be laying all sorts of peculiar eggs—little blue ones shaped like
anvils and all whatnot—until they figure out what Dr. Joe is egg-
ing them on toward.)

Would the Vandepopuliegg just kind of gloop out? I wondered.
Wouldn't that be kind of messy? Dr. Joe says it ain't so. Inside an
eggshell is a soft, pliant membrane. That would contain the egg
solids. I supposed aloud that chickens would be grateful to lay
something softer. That ain't so either, says Dr. Joe. Chickens, as far
as anyone can tell, are feeling no pain when they lay eggs, he said.
(Has anyone ever asked—*really* asked?) That shoots my idea for a
French existential novel based entirely on the Sisyphean struggles
and inner sufferings of a chicken laying an egg, to have been (more
or less) onomatopoetically titled *Oeuf!*

As befits a curmudgeonly social critic, I have to say it will cause
me great sorrow if the eggshell goes the way of all flesh. Walking
on eggs is difficult enough as things stand. And cracking an egg
into a pan is something we do with a certain unobserved pleasure,
I'll hazard. (On New Year's Day and sundry other hung-over
mornings, of course, a silent egg would be a Vandepopulieresend.)
What's more, in this ever-shifting, transient society, where it is not
unusual to see a chicken going braless (okay, so I lied about not
mentioning them again), there is something reassuring about the
way an egg feels and looks, no? I wonder if these new quivering,
nebulous globules will even deserve to be called something as
punch and definitive as "egg." They should wear a lesser name.
How about "ehh"?

I know what the perspicacious reader is saying right now. He or
she is saying, "How long have I been asleep?" Ha-ha. No, no, the
perspicacious reader is saying, "Does this writer idly scan gazettes
for chicken developments, or does he' ever go out and work the

streets and grapple firsthand with the very pith and marrow of chicken existence?"

So let me tell you about the day one of my readers, a Hartford commuter, called me to tell of a wild chicken he had seen scrambling around the median strip of Interstate 86 for several days running (or scrambling).

"Does it sleep there? Maybe it doesn't sleep. It's just a stupid chicken," he speculated, as if the chicken's karma were such a pale, untaxing thing that there was little need to shut it down for a rest.

I knew better. And I have often thought that Hartford needs a shady, legendary animal on the order of Champ or Nessie or Bigfoot, so I hightailed it out to the alleged habitat of the Hartford highway chicken. I parked my car off the highway and walked to the edge. There, parading on the median, was a brown-and-white chicken. Traffic whizzed by at death-defying speeds, inches from the beast's pinfeathers. It was unfazed.

Behold a heroic bird, I told myself.

I walked over to a nearby construction site. That part of the highway has been under construction for about eight years, in an ongoing effort, I believe, to simulate the landscape and atmosphere of Mars, the better to attract science-fiction movie producers. The workers at the site denied seeing a chicken, possibly because their eyes tended to gravitate toward the cranes swinging huge, deadly chunks of concrete and metal through the air in terrifying arcs.

My interviews with them proceeded haltingly. One guy pointed to the tape recorder I was holding out to him and said, "You're supposed to tell somebody when you tape them. I'll take my crowbar and mash that thing up for you."

"Ha-ha-ha," I said nervously, to prove I enjoyed his joke.

I finally located a relatively genial worker named Ed, who said the chicken had been on the median for weeks.

"He's very hip to traffic," said Ed. "He never crosses the yellow line."

Rumor among the construction crews had it that the chicken had been living in the vicinity for months, said Ed.

"Have you guys given the chicken a name?" I asked.

"Lucky," said Ed.

"What does the chicken live on?" I asked some other workers.

"Exhaust fumes," said one guy.

I went home and found myself worrying about Lucky. I called the Humane Society. The guy there said they were already on Lucky's trail, but their operatives had been unable to snare the wily chicken.

The following day, however, he called me back and said, in the crisp tones of a bureaucrat addressing the news media, "We have the bird in hand."

"Is it worth two in the bush?" I couldn't help asking.

"Yes," he said, and didn't elaborate.

"Are you going to rehabilitate the chicken?" I asked.

"We'll send her to a farm."

I had mixed feelings about this solution. No sooner do I discover a wild, mysterious chicken doing a dance of death with Hartford's highway commuters than it is captured in a humane dragnet. On the other hand, this is no ordinary chicken. I would not be surprised to learn that they haven't built a farm that can hold Lucky.

I will not involve myself further in Lucky's case. A bard does not meddle in the affairs of men and chickens. He is content to make sure that the chicken's deeds do not pass unsung.

And still of a summer's morn, they say, when the road is
    jammed with traffic,
When the dump trucks seem quite elephantine and the cranes
    are most giraffic,
When the asphalt's a ribbon of autos, locked in the gridlock's
    grip,
The Highwaychicken comes pecking,
Pecking, pecking.
The Highwaychicken comes pecking, up the median strip.

What Animals Don't Tell People

"If a lion could speak," wrote Wittgenstein, "we would not understand it."

Well . . . surely there would be a few subjects of mutual interest to the lion and us.

I'm not saying a lion could sit right in on "Agronsky and Company" and never miss a beat. I'm not even saying a lion would, on the dullest day of its life, want to. On the other hand, if a discussion of wage-price supports was, in the lion's opinion, bogging down, the lion might eat George Will, which would liven things up.

Frankly, I sometimes think, especially while attending parties, that I would have more things to talk about with a lion than I do with quite a few people.

In this chapter, I will explore the question of whether it is possible for an animal to know a language.

When I say "language," I mean it in the way that Schleiermacher used "language" in his 1887 essay, "This Is What I Mean When I Say 'Language.'" And when I say "know," I use it in the sense of Kant's classic formulation, "I know you are fooling around with the chauffeur." And, of course, when I say "and," I mean it in the sense of "Starsky 'and' Hutch," exclusive of whatever application that might have to "surf 'and' turf." But perhaps the dilemma of the cognitive linguist can be best summed up in the work of Dr. K. Sirrah, who argued in 1933 that he could not think clearly if there were going to be quotation marks around every dag-blasted word.

Some of the most stunning research concerning animal communications has involved the lowly ant. The mystery of ant communication has fascinated experts through the ages, yet one studies ants at one's peril.

So writes Cornell entomologist Fiona Dashweiler in the preface of her book *Aaaaaa*. Dashweiler explains that the ants in her neighborhood routinely broke into her study at night and destroyed the parts of her manuscript they did not like, which is why her book consists entirely of a preface.

Dashweiler says the ants were especially resentful when she went into New York City to discuss them at long lunches with her publisher. She hypothesizes that ants resent it when *anybody* eats *anything* without them.

She further postulates that any given ant, at any given moment, knows exactly "who is eating what" everywhere in the world and how long it would take it (the ant) to get to each of these eating sites and whether or not there would be anything left for it by the time it arrived.

Dashweiler, who was hospitalized for nervous exhaustion before the publication of her book, concludes on a shrill note: "I have never, in all my born days, come across a more ungrateful, messy, arrogant, wretched, sordid, nasty bunch of little animals with no regard for common— Hey, get *out* of here! I'm serious! *Get off my desk, you! Ouch!*"

Other scientists have made deeper inroads. Professor Boyce Misericordia of Jarvis State began his research into ant language by reclassifying ants into four new groups.

1. Big Ones. These are ants whose lone function is to be slightly larger than ants are commonly thought to be and thus give pause to anyone who chances upon them.

2. Draggers. These are ants who are always hauling huge chunks of stuff around kind of aimlessly. Misericordia postulates that two draggers could haul an object "the size of David Crosby" from Lake Tahoe to Denver, but he doubts they would want to.

3. Wallowers. These are ants who are "always climbing around on some disgusting thing or other," Misericordia writes.

4. Molders, Corporals, Scones, and Key Grips. These are ants whom Misericordia always sees out of the corner of his eye, but never when he looks straight at them, forcing him to conclude that they are watching him and trying to figure out what he does for a living.

Misericordia's classification system has truly opened up the boundaries of ant language research, and his own findings in that area, although thought-provoking, are somewhat tarnished by his insistence that, on several occasions when they thought no one was watching, he saw ants peel off their black costumes to reveal beautiful shining little people who resembled, to an astonishing degree, Joey Heatherton.

More reliable findings have come from Dr. I. L. Putawarana of the Eastern Baptist Cybernetics Institute, who has published his findings in *Nnnnng: The Journal of Ant Thought.*

Putawarana developed equipment with which to tune in on the actual thoughts of ants, through a satellite dish shaped like a giant picnic basket. He monitored the device for more than four years before finally picking up these thoughts from a nearby ant:

Run run run run what's that run run climb on something fetid run run run now climb on some virgin white pudding run run whoo hey run WHAT'S THAT RUN HEY RUN RUN OOooowwrr . . .

Putawarana writes in the accompanying notes, "At that moment it was an unsplendid occurrence that my worthless son Rajiv happened upon the ant and squished from it the very substance of its life."

Ant experiments, multifarious though they may be, can shed only a limited amount of light on our subject because, as so many theorists have remarked, "Who cares about ants?" Besides, I made up all that stuff about them.

However, mention animal language and someone will want to discuss those gorillas who speak in sign language.

Out in California, there are two of them. A gorilla named Michael, who has said things like "Trouble Mike strangle alligator squash." And a gorilla named Koko, who has said things like "Koko know elephant devil."

The gorillas have come in for quite a bit of criticism from people who doubt that they (the gorillas) actually know what they're saying. I don't know. I sometimes endure a whole cocktail party waiting for someone to say anything as interesting to me as "Trouble Mike strangle alligator squash." I would be a more rousing conversationalist if such lively guests were present. It's even more impressive when you consider that these gorillas live in California.

And on how many evenings would the television newscast be vastly improved if the anchorperson simply said, "Koko know elephant devil. Thank you. We'll be back at eleven"?

My personal experience in animal language has involved pigs. I have conducted a long-running experiment in which I have tried to strike up a conversation with the pigs who live on a local farm where I buy my (chicken) eggs. I don't imagine that I get the full force of the pigs' point of view, but such noises as they feel moved to make are enlightening.

Still, I believe I am regarded by my human peers as an eccentric. At parties, I will sometimes interject, "I spoke with some pigs today. They strung themselves out in a line on the other side of the pen and stared quite fixedly at me, and I found myself wondering what it was they—"

"Yeah, great, so anyway Eunice is just totally hacked off about this, and of course you can't get anybody to come in for less than two hundred and fifty dollars, so . . ." the party people go on about their business, which is what people like to go on about.

I tried to share some of these perspectives with my dog Roy when he was a newly acquired puppy and thus only beginning to form language skills.

The only thing Roy knew at the time was his name. He was named after my favorite writer, Roy Blount, Jr.

In those days, I often had occasion to be thankful that my favorite writer was not, let us say, Baudelaire. It would have depleted my ego in certain ways to stand outdoors in the October moonlight beseeching thusly: "Come on, Baudelaire, do your potty."

Besides, it is simply no good, making a dog bear the weight of a

French poet's name—a peevish, sybaritic poet at that. Had I not studiously avoided French literature all my life, we could have been in a terrible fix.

In any case, at my wife's suggestion, we made a linguistic adjustment in the potty command. We told Roy, "Do your business."

My wife is a psychotherapist, and her choice of words probably reflects the Freudian principle (if I understand Freud) that money is the adult's substitute for excrement or that excrement is the infant's first experience with tender, legal or otherwise (probably I don't understand Freud). Certainly, there were some very late, chilly nights when I congratulated Roy for his business as heartily as if he had produced a Krugerrand.

In my own case, constant repetition of this mantra (sometimes, when Roy seemed to be in need of extra exhortation, I would simply cry, "Business, business, business!" while flapping my arms in the cold night air) gradually deepened my ambivalence toward business, so that now, at parties, when I meet someone who says, "I'm in business," it conjures up a completely different image in my mind than the person had intended. (I do not know what to make, in this context, of the quote by worm fancier Edward J. Salliant, cited in the chapter "You, Your Yard, and You Again": "My business is not worm poop. It's financial planning.")

I believe if you put the whole issue to one of those signing gorillas, he or she might remark, "I a Koko, standard and poor toilet devil."

While I was pondering these matters, someone showed me a press release about Israeli kibbutz farmers who had managed to keep wild gazelles from destroying their crops by spreading "fresh lion droppings." Gazelles make it their business to avoid areas where lions make their business. (If a lion could speak, it would certainly insist on some new coinage, such as "lion placings," on the grounds that it never did anything so, so . . . unstudied as a dropping.)

The farmers were getting the droppings from a nearby game park. They worked out a deal to swap lion food for lion waste, which seemed to me like good business.

I tried to rough this out for Roy, tried to make him see the vast panoply of international interests into which he might, in some way, fit: farmers producing food for lions who produce droppings that frighten gazelles so that more food can be produced for humans who write for newspapers which are placed all over the kitchen floor until their dogs learn to take their business elsewhere.

I was running through the whole deal with him late one night in the ninth week of his life, when he suddenly looked up at me and said, "Does this mean that we could, theoretically, place a specific monetary value on a unit of gazelle fright?"

As I say, he was only eight weeks old, so my feeling was this was just some loose talk he picked up from the pigs.

Science Trudges On

It will have occurred to certain readers that there is not a lot of genuine, reliable scientific information about animals in this book.

I am not that sort of scientist. If I am any sort, I am the Einstein type of scientist. By which I mean that I have lots of interesting, but not very practical, things to say about the universe.

In fact, it really broke my heart when they revealed a while back that Einstein was not a potatohead in his school days. This was a pleasing fiction in which we potatoheads used to take a great deal of solace and refuge.

All through school, I comforted myself with the notion that Einstein had been every bit as dumb in science as I was. I think I may have even tried out that line of thought on a few teachers.

Einstein's duncehood was just something everybody agreed about, right? I never saw it written down anywhere. That gave you a great deal of flexibility. On a real bad day, you could afford to imagine that Einstein sat numbly with a sort of glazed look in his eyes until the age of twenty-three, when he just started spouting relativity and quasars to beat the band.

Then I had to read "Einstein Revealed as Brilliant in Youth" in the New York *Times* Science section. (Have you ever noticed how much truly dispiriting information there is in that section? Every week, it's something like "Scientists Notice Universe Shredding to Pieces; Will Be Pretty Much Kaput by 1989.")

Seems to me these killjoys owe us some psychological compensation, if they insist on taking Einstein away. Maybe circulate the idea that Leonardo da Vinci failed everything except gym, all the way through high school, that he hung around outside the Florence drugstore reading comic books with a match in his teeth until he was nineteen. Or that Thomas Edison couldn't *change* a light bulb, much less invent one, as a kid, that Edison sold *Grit* and was so shiftless it took him seventeen years to win a Schwinn bicycle.

But I'm not holding my breath.

From time to time, we read of a new study proving that America is lagging behind rival nations in the sciences. A recent article delighted me by complaining that some of our students are learning a lot of theory but have no idea of how to apply any of it to real life.

Speaking as a person for whom a lack of practical scientific knowledge has been absolutely crucial in becoming the animal expert I am today . . . speaking as that person . . . I am obliged to say that it took so long to establish whom I was speaking as that I forgot what I had intended to say.

I'll say this: The only way to learn anything practical about the real world in science class is to use the Socratic method.

Socrates, you will recall, tended to wander around the landscape with a bunch of guys in caftans. Socrates would pick up a rock and ask the guys, "What is a rock?"

The guys would all kind of murmur and then one of them, mayhaps Paragorikes, would step forward and say, "A rock is that which is hard, insensible, and not attached to the earth."

Socrates would arch his eyebrows and say, "Ah, but is that not also true of an actuary's heart?"

The guys would all squint and shake their heads appreciatively. Then everybody would knock off and go out for stuffed grape leaves.

In today's fast-paced world, this is no longer a practical way to educate anyone except University of Georgia football players. In our race for technological supremacy, we can ill afford to have our science students spend six weeks kicking around the essential differences between, say, a hamster and a pinecone.

We have been forced to move on to classroom experimentation. The basic scientific experiment—from which all others somehow derive their spirit—involves setting fire to a piece of paper, dropping it in a milk bottle, placing a hard-boiled egg on top of the milk bottle, and watching the egg be sucked down. No one has any idea what principle this illustrates or of what use it could be to anyone but a constipated and adventurous chicken. It seems like something that might have been discovered at the tail end of a boozy science-teacher office party. Anyway, most states require that it be demonstrated no fewer than twenty-eight times to every student passing through the public schools.

Meanwhile, of course, Japanese second-graders are being taught to make semiconductors out of gimp.

Animals regard science with great misapprehension, since it rarely works out in their favor. I read a couple of years back about a bunch of scientists who placed—Lord knows why—a zebra embryo in the womb of a regular old horse at the Louisville zoo. Imagine the horse's consternation, months later, when she gave birth to an op-art baby. This is the kind of thing I mean.

I feel obliged to tell you a little bit about my scientific background so you will know whom you're dealing with on some of the heady scientific issues in this book.

I received the bulk of my training from the famed scientist Mr. Pritchard, who taught an eighth-grade class in Setting Small, Noxious Chemical Fires and Weighing the Charred Remains on a Bead Scale. This, of course, represents a shrewd modification of The Basic Experiment, a modification in which several new principles are embraced: 1. Not wasting perfectly good eggs. 2. Weighing things (thus creating the illusion of accountability). 3. Hardly anybody makes milk bottles anymore.

The bead scales were issued to us at the start of the year, and Mr. Pritchard stressed that they were like invalid aunts and would go completely out of whack if treated with anything short of fanatical delicacy, which made me so nervous that I dropped mine on the floor and was unable to learn anything about the universe for the rest of the year.

And so it was that I was introduced to the two primary unfairnesses of science.

The first one is that the competent students always become each other's partners instead of pairing up with us potatoheads to pull us along.

The second one is that the object of science class is to make the experiments come out exactly the same way they have the last 78,293 times they were performed by others. No credit is given to the innovative student who is able to disprove the most closely held tenets of science, day in and day out.

Mr. Pritchard was keen on slide rules. Today's students have never heard of slide rules because they have grown intellectually fat and lazy by using little machines which actually provide them with answers, as opposed to slide rules, which are primarily meant to illustrate, in an especially vexing way, the futility of human effort. For all you kids who missed out on this fun, let me explain: A slide rule is two pieces of wood, each painted with random, illegible numbers and ingeniously fitted together so that a young, inquiring mind can slide the middle part to create precisely the right-sized space through which to inquire (read "peek") at the paper of one of the kids who refused to be his lab partner.

Having given Mr. Pritchard ample reason to consider joining his brother-in-law's Amway franchise, I moved on to biology, where the seeds of my expertise in animal life were sown. In biology, we were encouraged to rain havoc and destruction down upon the lives of helpless microorganisms and to cut open rats who had been dead for a long, long time.

Now, this latter activity strikes me as one with practical application in everyday life. In my adult life, whenever a doctor says to me something like "This whaddayacallit, spleen, has got to go," or "I'm fixing to take and hit your pancreas with this here ball peen hammer," or "Were you aware that your islets of Langerhans have arranged themselves in the image of the fourth face of Vishnu?" I try to summon up the image of what the particular organ in question looked like in the extremely dead rat. I find I am able to black out from fear and revulsion almost immediately, which has gone a long way toward making me a better patient.

The area of science which seems to produce the least amount of practical information is, of course, astronomy. This, I believe, is because astronomers are pretty much guessing about what is out there.

Outer space is an enormous place, more than fifty times the size of Nebraska. Big hunks of stuff are whirling around in it, getting in each other's way and smacking into things.

Once in a while, something comes zooming within a few hundred miles of earth, and astronomers are obliged to pretend they know what it is and that they knew it was coming all along. But you never hear them talking about these comets and eclipses and meteor showers until pretty much the last minute, do you?

Still, you can't blame them. How many grants would they get if they went around saying, "Jeez, it's so big out there, with jillions of asteroids whooshing around. Who can keep track of it all?"?

In Socrates' day, experts were more honest. They never knew what was happening, and when something such as an eclipse came along, it scared the living daylights (hence the expression) out of them.

And there were a lot more eclipses back then—a couple a week during the bad season. The ancients built Stonehenge just to take their minds off the whole nerve-wracking business.

To understand how truly bankrupt astronomy is, try this simple home simulation of a solar eclipse.

To represent the sun, place a beach ball on your dinner table. To represent the moon, place a chick-pea-sized piece of green cheese on the table. To represent the earth, place an apple (we find Granny Smith works the best) near the green cheese.

To the apple, glue lots of little teeny-weeny people holding up eensy-weensy pieces of cardboard with holes pricked in them.

Okay, now put the little piece of cheese in between the apple and the beach ball. Are you telling me the people on the apple can't see the beach ball?

So much for what astronomers know. For a more realistic picture of outer space, put lots of rocks and tennis balls and kiwi fruit and pork chops and any eggs you haven't sucked into milk bottles on the table along with the original three things. Then train four industrial-powered fans on the whole shebang. (This is called the Big Shebang Theory.) And have a couple of brutish friends whack the sides of the table with sledgehammers.

See how everything careens around in terrifying, chaotic arcs? That's outer space. Eventually, the apple will roll off the table and into a dark corner. That's an eclipse. If nobody picks the apple up, it's Roto-Rooter time for one and all.

Some serious theorists have proposed a modified scenario called, in honor of the "Dog Star," the Sirius Theory.

To illustrate it, put your dog up on the table with all of the other stuff. Roll the apple at the dog. The dog will snatch up the apple and hold it in the darkness of its jaws. That explains eclipses, not to mention the way your stomach sometimes lurches around your rib cage for no reason at all. When the dog notices the pork chop, it releases the apple. (Of course, for this theory to be true, certain parts of the world would be blanketed with dog breath, pitted with teeth marks, and splattered with animal saliva, which would go a long way toward explaining certain earthly phenomena, such as Worcester, Massachusetts.)

What has all this got to do with animals? Precious little. But it gives you renewed sympathy for animals in the grip of science. Take rats. Getting carved up by nauseated teenagers is perhaps the end which awaits them, but not before a succession of other indignities. I read a couple of years ago about a UCLA psychological study in which rats were driven to drink.

No kidding. The rats were given a choice of water or some kind of alcoholic beverage. . . . Gee, here would seem to be the place for a rat cocktail with a funny name, but I'm having some trouble thinking one up. Harvey Wallbanger would be sort of funny if it were rabbits. I welcome your suggestions, for the unlikely event that this book goes into a second printing. Send them to Andy Rooney, c/o CBS News, New York, N.Y.

Anyway, the rats had a choice of water or hootch. The idea was to see whether they would voluntarily knock a few back.

The rats were given ample food, a recreational area—I'm not sure what that entailed; maybe tiny hot tubs and ratball courts— and very little of what a rat would consider stress. No cats, no traps, no mazes, no memos, no demands for greater productivity, no life insurance salesmen, no MTV. In short, no rat race.

What happened was uncanny.

First off, 25 percent of the rats chose to flat out abstain from the firewater. A veritable Rodent's Christian Temperance Union. And about 10 percent immediately became problem juicers, often going for the first nip of the day right after yawning and stretching.

Here's where it gets really weird: The rest of the rats became social drinkers. They got into the habit of drinking about two hours before mealtime. Every three or four days, however, they would have a little party and get really hammered. After that, they'd ease up on the sauce for a while.

I suppose the next step for UCLA is to simulate human living conditions a bit more exactly. They probably have someone making little lampshades for rats to put on their heads at parties and little ice bags for the rats to put on their heads the next day. And rat briefcases. And a little rat commuter train with a bar car.

Picture it.

Rat 1: "Tough day at the maze?"

Rat 2: "You know it. Got a new honcho there—some punk kid gunning for his master's. The putz is really on my case. 'Find the cheese, follow the light, press the lever, no, not *that* lever.' Wham! I get a shock that would light up the Seagram building. Speaking of which, I think I'll have another drinkie-winkie."

Rat 1: "You really oughta ease up on that stuff. Your eyes are red, and you're as white as a ghost."

Rat 2: "So what? I'm a rat! I'm supposed to look like that! You know, you're not exactly Mel Gibson yourself. Now get off my tail, willya?"

Rat 1: "You're a mean drunk, Charlie. You really turn into a human."

Rat 2: "Ya ya ya."

I question whether this experiment has any practical application in real life. I guess it could conceivably be useful in the difficult task of getting pandas to breed. They could hold a panda office party for all the zoo pandas in the United States, serve bamboo stalks and dip, Singapore slings, etc. After the pandas got a few paws to the wind, they'd probably start sneaking off with each other's mates. Not an optimal situation, but it might be the best we can do.

If the pandas got really plastered, they might start telling off the scientists for messing around with them. That alone would be worth it.

And as a sobriety test, we could make the pandas try to do the egg-in-the-milk-bottle experiment.

Men Who Hate Cats and the Women Who Love Them and the Cats Who . . .

Woman: Do you love my cat?
Man: Well . . . no, but I love you. Isn't that enough?
Woman: You don't love my cat?

* * *

What is it about men and cats? About men and women and cats?

The three are often poised in an uneasy balance. In some of the best circumstances, this is true. In other cases, only the cat is poised. The cat is always poised.

A woman will love a cat. It is beautiful, composed, and . . . well, not exactly loyal. But it is there for her on the lonely Saturday night, when nobody else is.

Enter the man. The man was not brought up to like cats. Cats do not embrace what the man considers to be manly virtues. Cats do not embrace anybody. Cats are shifty, insouciant, meanspirited, the man thinks.

The woman worries that the man is displacing his resentment of feminine nature onto the cat. You would be surprised (or maybe you wouldn't) at how often cats get dragged into feminist thinking. And they have to be dragged. Cats are not willing partners to ideologies.

The man worries that the woman admires the cat's indifference to him.

The cat . . . Well, who knows?

One day, the cat gets up on the sofa next to the man, stares fixedly at him for five minutes, leaps up, and bites the side of his head.

This scene repeats itself every day, somewhere in America. And if it does not, it might just as well. That is not the point. We are not sure what the point is. We are trying to go out to the very frontier of human and cat affairs and see exactly what the point is.

I was asked to perform this public service by a newspaper. In that context, I felt obliged to interview people. I heard things that would curl your hair, unless you were a cat. I don't know who the man and woman who keep talking back and forth in italics are, but everybody else you will encounter here is a real person whose name has not been changed.

*   *   *

Woman: *You do love my cat?*
Man: *I'm learning to get along with the cat.*
Woman: *What does it say about us that you can't love my cat?*

*   *   *

Case #1. I call this The Case of . . . to tell the truth, I haven't gotten around to thinking up snappy names for my cases. Some rainy day I will spread them all out in front of me, and if a cat doesn't walk on them first, name them.

This case concerns my friend Barry, who, as a callow youth, saw no intrinsic difference between cats and soccer balls. This is the attitude of lot of guys.

One day, in adult life, this very same Barry person calls me up out of the blue to ask me if I will cat-sit for him. I say yes, because this is obviously some kind of joke.

Turns out Barry has gone and got himself a woman friend who comes with cat included. He shows up at my door holding a large paper bag into which he peers and says, "Time to wake up, kitty!" Whereupon, he lets go of the bag, which falls to the floor with an enormous thud.

He looks up at me and murmurs, "She doesn't travel well."

Of course, it turns out the bag contains the cat's food. This is what former cat-hating guys do when they are going soft on cats. They turn toward violent humor as a means of suppressing their inner confusion. See Freud on this. (I have no damn idea what Freud says about it, but it seemed like a good idea to mention him.)

Anyway, coming up my walk behind Barry is his nervous-looking woman friend carrying an even more nervous-looking cat. The cat—named Doodle or Gerkins or something—is deposited. They leave.

I regard the cat and affect my best Dickensian orphan-master's sneer. "Ye know, we don't like spoiled cats here. Ye'll be expected t' work fer yer keep!"

The cat gives me a hollow look, slinks off behind a dresser, and pretty much stays there for the whole weekend.

TO BE CONTINUED . . .

* * *

Woman: Do you love my cat?
Man: Well, I love your cat, because it's an animal, and I love animals."
Woman: Do you love my cat?
Man: Why do you keep saying that?

* * *

And now the thrilling conclusion to Case #1.

Months later, I run into Barry. He and the woman friend have called it quits. She has moved back to the Midwest.

"Well, you're rid of the cat anyway," I offer.

"No, Puffin [or Darkins] stayed with me."

"What?"

"Oh yeah, I've been born again."

Damned if he hasn't.

"You start to talk to the animal in this affected voice," he admits, a little sheepishly (not to drag sheep into this). "It sleeps with you, follows you around, looks at you with pathetic eyes."

He refers to his old attitude toward cats as "machismo."

Machismo. Jeez.

*   *   *

Woman: Do you love my cat?
Man: Look, you do nothing with the cat. I feed the cat. I play with the
cat. I try to put the cat out at night but it runs all over the place, and I
wind up barking, you should pardon the expression, my shins on the coffee
table, and then at 2 A.M. it decides it does want to go out and wakes me up.
You sleep through this. You have virtually no involvement with the cat.
What do you want from me?
Woman: Why can't you say you love my cat?

*   *   *

The thing is, Barry is no isolated case.

Case #2. I found a guy named Dr. Stanton Wolfe, whose name was, from a cat's point of view, one strike against him. Wolfe was an oral surgeon who had always loved animals but hated cats. "I thought they were dumb, aloof, nonresponsive. They just got fed and things."

Wolfe was finally persuaded to get a cat, for the sake of his kids and his wife. ("She needed something to stroke other than me," he said.) The cat is named Pinter (Mrs. Wolfe is of a theatrical bent), and Wolfe likes it. He rationalizes this: "He's part dog. He's very affectionate and has much greater dimensions than I had suspected cats had. He's even trainable."

Dimensions . . . hmmmm.

This just in: An assistant professor at the University of Pennsylvania School of Veterinary Medicine conducted a study of attitudes in cat owners. Eighty-four percent of the respondents were women. On the other hand, the 16 percent who were men did not demonstrate any major differences from the women in their attitude toward cats. Make of that what you will.

Meanwhile, I found, in the Yellow Pages, under "Catteries," the Sherwood Cattery in Guilford, Connecticut. I called it and found myself speaking with Florence Sherwood Kanoffe, proprietress and, I would hazard, chief catter.

"I've been with cats for thirty years, if that means anything," said Florence Sherwood Kanoffe.

I told her I was sure it meant something.

Men, said Ms. F. S. Kanoffe, sometimes consider a cat "a woman's plaything" (Author's note: And the same might be said of how cats consider men), until the men get to know a cat. "Then, it's the men who go overboard."

A better reporter would have followed right up and asked Florence Sherwood Kanoffe what exactly she meant by "go overboard," but I think we can all form our own mental pictures of men buying cat toys, talking about their cats' "dimensions," and perhaps even taking their cats to the cat cosmetologist to have its colors done.

And indeed, it struck me that beauticians often know the deepest secrets of their clients. Another trip to the Yellow Pages acquainted me with Bubbles Dog Grooming ("We Also Do Cats"). I phoned and spoke to Susan Charette, who told me "a lot of your single men are getting cats."

Why would my single men be getting cats? I wondered. Because they don't like coming home to empty houses, Ms. Charette explained, and cats are less work than dogs. Also less work than women, I thought.

In fact, while I was researching this story, I got so I would ask just about anybody I happened to meet for their thoughts on the subject. A woman who had worked in the state prison system told me that a cat, in a men's prison, is considered one of the ultimate treasures—to be hidden away and lavished with morsels of food.

I also heard about a new, arguably utopian breed of cat, which I drove many miles to inspect. It is called the Ragdoll cat.

To picture the Ragdoll cat, you would do well to remember how Charles Schulz, many years ago, tried to introduce a cat into the comic strip "Peanuts."

The cat, which had no name, was always seen draped sleepily over the arms of a curly-haired girl named Frieda.

The cat was eventually written out of the strip because (I'm guessing) there was nothing for it to do and because Snoopy, insofar as he is willful, capricious, and mildly disdainful of humans, was a lot more like a cat than like a dog anyway. (Actually, my wife, a psychotherapist, theorizes that Snoopy is popular because he resembles a breast. I don't know how that might fit into the

overall scheme of this article, but if there's anyone out there casting around for a doctoral thesis topic . . .)

Anyway, the Ragdoll is life imitating a cartoon failure. The
breed is the product of some felicitous messing around with several
cat gene pools, including the Turkish Angora and the sacred cat of
Burma. (The latter, I gather, is a breed, rather than an individual
cat.) The Ragdoll is a cat which will hang limply and agreeably
from one's arms. A Ragdoll likes to lie on its back with its arms and
legs outstretched in a nothing-to-hide gesture.

A utopian cat?

I visited with a Ragdoll breeder who told me the cats have never
scratched her. They are not allowed outdoors because, with their
Gomer Pyle personalities, they would attempt to befriend assorted
predators and sharpies of the non-utopian wild.

The breeder told me the Ragdoll even practices Lamaze. At
birthing time, mama drags hubby to the delivery site, where he
kind of presides over things, cleans up the new arrivals, etc. None
of the usual pacing back and forth on the other side of the door
taking catnip. The first time around, the breeder didn't know this,
so she segregated the expectant mother, who to all appearances *held
it* until hubby was brought to her side.

Yow. A utopian cat?

The breed is only twenty years old. Kind of makes you wonder
what's waiting down the line. By the year 2000, we could be looking at a cat who collects for UNICEF on Halloween, who helps
elderly mice cross the street, who jumps on a live vacuum cleaner
to save the rest of the platoon.

Could this be the solution to all the problems we are discussing
in this public-service article? I don't know. I'm not sure how men
—or women, for that matter—would feel about a cat who was
better than they. The cats I have known have always been infi-
nitely more venal and ignoble than I. They have all had a few good
qualities, which they generally regarded as weaknesses. On days
when I have felt particularly abased, they have made for a sordid
type of good company.

There is also the issue of price. These cats start at around $275
per. It might be hard for a man to maintain the necessary psycho-

logical advantage over such an expensive cat. He could wind up feeling like a $75,000 manager coaching a $1.2 million left fielder.

Even in a theoretical utopia, a cat so far removed, karma-wise, from the very nut of cathood might rankle folks who were big on Platonic ideals. You'd get discussion groups forming over this furred apple of discord, to the neglect of the windmills, the kelp beds, the ginseng refinery.

No, this cat is not the answer. We have ventured down a blind alley. We must return to the thoroughfare of cats *qua* cats.

* * *

Woman: Do you love my cat?
Man: What is this "your cat"?
Woman: Well . . . it is my cat.
Man: It likes me better.

* * *

Which is not to say that there aren't some diehards among the men and cats. While blazing the trail into this new area of journalism, I gazed straight into the soft white underbelly of human and cat nature. Yessir, I heard some stories, let me tell you.

Talked to a woman whose father threw a cat named Ralph out of a second-story window. The cat lived to tell the tale but didn't. It became the oldest cat in Hartford, Connecticut, by this woman's account. I don't know how that was arrived at. They have actuarial tables on everything in Hartford.

Talked to an ailurophobic ad man named Jay Durepo, who told me he once broke off a relationship over a cat. "I said it was break up or kill the cat. We broke up."

Durepo prides himself on his inability to see the greater dimensions of cats.

"A cat is the lowest form of life that has ever trod the earth," he said. "Also, I don't trust anything that can climb higher than me. I don't like to come into someone's house and see one up on the refrigerator, looking down at me and twitching its tail."

Durepo also flat out rejected the machismo concept: "All this nonsense about how men who don't like cats are insecure . . . I'm incredibly secure."

He sounded secure.

We turn now to Case # . . . actually, I have been lax about even numbering these cases. Let's say #7. Jim Sorrell, a compliance officer for a big insurance company, lives at swords' points with the cat of the woman he loves.

"It's a very unfriendly cat," he told me glumly. "You can't get near it. It will scrunch down and snarl."

Sorrell dislikes cats as a species. "They're sneaky. I love dogs. They appreciate what you do for them. Cats don't."

Sorrell and the cat have very little to do with each other.

"It makes no noise," he said, not one whit less glumly. "It just slinks around."

Still, Sorrell is not one to draw a Durepo line in the dirt. "There's room enough for everybody," he says, sounding, well, almost convinced.

Have cats been utterly blameless in all this? Of course not.

Consider Case #29, the story of Janet Brown, who runs a school for the performing arts. As a single woman, Janet lived in a one-room flat with a Siamese cat named Morris.

"He slept on my neck at night, and we ate tuna and Cheez-Its out of the same containers," she recalled. "It was that kind of a relationship." (Author's note: I think we can safely lump "that kind of a relationship" and "going overboard" into the same general category.)

Janet added, "I later found out that he would go to parties on the floor below [presumably having waited for Janet's neck to fall asleep] and drink beer, inhale marijuana fumes, and eat potato chips."

Okay, I would like to pause here and apologize for the fact that some of the stories in this chapter have been kind of pedestrian. I did not permit myself to make up anything for this public-service article, so I was kind of forced to live with what was out there. However, as we re-join this particular story, you are going to see that I did not come up completely dry in my drilling. Obsessive, possessive love is all the rage these days as a pop pathology, and you are about to read, for the first time between two covers, the story of a cat who wouldn't let go.

And now, back to Janet, who started dating a guy named Paul. Morris did not hide his feelings about Paul. If Paul sat on Janet's bed, which doubled as a couch, Morris would insert himself under the covers of the bed and burrow, molelike, toward Paul. We have already pointed out that Morris had a substance-abuse problem, so it is possible that he thought he could not be seen. When he arrived at Paul's body, he would bite up through the bedspread and into Paul's flesh. I swear this is true, and if you're interested in the made-for-TV movie rights, give me a call.

Whenever Paul showed signs of leaving the apartment, Morris would race to the door to show him out. When Paul went to the door, Morris would run down the hall ahead of him and on down the stairs, ushering, ushering, until Paul was out. Then Morris would get up on his hind legs and peer out the window, savoring Paul's departure.

Paul was no Durepo. He extended olive branches to Morris, but what is a cat going to do with an olive branch? Even when Paul and Janet got married and moved to a new apartment, Morris's hate burned ever bright. Like many a guerrilla before him, Morris hoped to whittle away at the enemy's confidence and eventually drive him off the homeland.

It is somehow not surprising that Paul suddenly began to exhibit terrible respiratory problems, which were diagnosed as an allergy to guess what. Janet was suddenly transformed into a woman whose fortunes were no less problematical than, let us say, Roxanne's. She searched her soul and Paul's sinuses (apostrophically) and decided to give Morris to her mother.

Grief-torn and, let us not forget, cut off cold turkey from marijuana and beer, Morris threw himself under the wheels of a car.

Cat journalism is not pretty.

*   *   *

Woman: Do you know what your cat did today?
Man: My cat?

*   *   *

I don't know about you, but I do not trust myself to go on much further with this public-service article. I would like to wrap it up but . . . Do you know what it needs? An expert of some kind.

But such a one is hard to find. There aren't a lot of tenured chairs in this sort of thing—not that I'm even precisely sure what this sort of thing might be called—at your major groves of academe.

Bless my soul, I did find a chap named Robert Steele, associate professor of psychology and women's studies at Wesleyan University. Better yet, Steele also volunteers for an agency which places mistreated or abandoned animals in new homes. With a little prodding, Steele held forth as though he had been waiting all of his life for someone to write a public-service article on this subject and interview him for it.

He has noticed the way women come to the animal shelter and make straight for the cats.

Steele said, "Men stand off like they're *gauging* something." (Dimensions?) He also observed that men often move in abrupt, violent ways, which frighten cats.

Steele thinks that "men really guard their emotions." And so do cats. Is it possible that the two groups are actually too much alike ever to trust each other?

Hmmm.

And yet, I told Steele, there is some other deep, archetypal deal here.

"That's right," he mused. "Cats have generally been associated with goddesses, and they have been the companions of witches and powerful women. Maybe there are some age-old resonances, somewhere down deep, having to do with women's secrets and cats' secrets. Men think: This is not my territory. Guess I'll go off and talk to the dog."

So hey, can I find quotable experts or what?

Steele and I agreed that men are changing, but . . . can they change enough for cats? And are cats going to meet them halfway? Or even one third?

Okay, that does it for this public-service article. Get the lights and cue the italic people.

* * *

Woman: You know, sometimes I think you love my cat more than you love me.

Man: Mmmmmmm?

If the Dinosaurs Were So Smart, Why Weren't They Rich?

For years, or at least for the better part of one resort season, the best minds in science clung to the theory known as Higginbotham's Uncertainty in considering the mystery of what killed the dinosaurs.

Higginbotham divided his theory into two parts.

Part One: He didn't know what killed the dinosaurs.

Part Two: He didn't care.

This is, of course, an oversimplification for purposes of condensation. Higginbotham could really go on about this, if given an opening.

Now, decades later, Higginbotham stands, discredited, with one hand in the air, as if hailing a taxi. A new generation of scientists, using computer technology, laser graphics, an Oster deluxe kitchen center, and many other labor-saving devices, has begun reconstructing this ancient puzzle to a point where the total picture emerges, except for one area in the middle which could be a cloud or some turkeys and also something down in the corner which might be a wagon wheel or . . . well, it's hard to say.

Scientists have complained bitterly that people who have used the age-old puzzle in the past have not always put all of its pieces back in the box when they were through.

One the leading lights of this new movement is Witold Murfreesboro, who has argued passionately that dinosaurs were not the plodding, slow-witted, cold-blooded reptiles they have been made out to be. Although Murfreesboro has supporters for his belief that dinosaurs were warm-blooded, few of them will accompany him to the extreme frontiers of his theories or even walk him to his car. Murfreesboro has argued at various times that dinosaurs hunted in packs, that they developed a primitive type of outdoor furniture, and that they were capable of astonishingly sophisticated plotting when it came to avoiding their in-laws over the holidays.

Murfreesboro has asked the best minds in science to consider regrouping dinosaurs into a new class of animals, to be called Livwirae, which would also include certain birds, ferrets, and television game-show hosts, but so far, serious consideration of the idea has been impeded by the convulsive laughter it seems to evoke (although not, we regret to add, among readers of this book).

The mass extinction of the dinosaurs some 13 million years ago continues to be a mystery, attributable in part to poor record keeping at the time.

Astrophysicist Anatole Alembique has concluded that an enormous death star hurtling through outer space killed the dinosaurs and that it will return sometime within the next 13 million years to rain fiery destruction down upon the earth, so that, in his view, "One should really think twice about opening one of those Individual Retirement Accounts."

Opponents of Alembique's theory argue that no astronomer has ever actually seen the death star, known in some circles as Nemesis. (In others, it is called Bernice.) Alembique has postulated that Nemesis would look like "a gigantic glazed doughnut on fire," but at a recent colloquium, he allowed as how that was basically a "lucky guess" on his part.

Dr. Hector Beeker thought he had seen the death star on one celebrated occasion and ran through his observatory (Hector's 1-Stop Observatory and Centrifuge out on Route 11) yelling "Eureka!" and "Whoo, whoo, here comes the death star!"

But subsequently he could not find it. He decided it had been a speck on his telescope lens. "Or something swimming around in my eye. Do you ever get those? Those amoeba-looking things?" he inquired at the 1984 Best Minds in Science Luau and Frisbee Toss.

This was considered par for the course with Beeker, who indeed had one of the best minds in science but would do things like polish and polish his telescope lens for hours and then leave a peanut-butter sandwich on it ten minutes later.

If Nemesis does indeed exist, theorists believe that it barges into our solar system once every 26 million years, jarring deadly comets loose from the Ooomygoodnessgracious Cloud, a galactic mass named for Fedor Ooomygoodnessgracious, who in 1963 persuaded the scientific world that his cloud existed by just nagging and nagging until everybody gave in.

What could be done to avert such a repeat occurrence? Somehow, Nemesis itself would have to be altered to render it harmless. Few theorists have any idea of how to make Nemesis a normal, harmless, itinerant star, but Jim at D'Onofrio's Exxon in Waterbury, Connecticut, offered the following assessment: "The dripping near the tail could be gasket problems, and the sparks over the top would mean she threw a rod. Until I get in there and start working, there's no way to tell how bad it's gonna be. You can let it ride for, oh, seventeen, maybe nineteen billion miles, but someday the nexus is gonna go, and that runs into some money."

Many of the scientists who reject the Nemesis theory hold that the dinosaurs died when they became stuck in enormous tar pits. The debate over this notion hinged at one time on the question of who, exactly, would be operating a tar pit 13 million years ago, when there was relatively little road construction going on.

And in 1974, Dr. Arturo Possum tested the hypothesis by constructing an enormous tar pit in his backyard and trying to get various "subjects" (primarily door-to-door canvassers) stuck in it.

"Most of them were able to get out when the weather turned cold," he reported somewhat ruefully at the 1978 Best Minds in Science International Synod and Dinner-Dance.

The Synod that year was marked by heated disputes between the two scholarly camps, and there were hard feelings after the death star proponents did "The Wave" during one of Possum's presentations.

Possum's revelations, on the other hand, did nothing to reassure Hans von Shagrin, who had one of the best minds but two of the worst ears in science. "How could dinosaurs, beasts who were in many cases three times the size of Raymond Burr, become stuck in carpets?" he continued to worry. "Even the deep pile in my sister-in-law's downstairs . . ."

And there, it would seem, is the great debate stuck as well, until new evidence is unearthed or people start returning each other's messages.

On the horizon looms the controversial Hofnagel-Minoso Stipulation, which posits that the dinosaurs died because they, or someone close to them, removed one or more of those DO NOT REMOVE UNDER PENALTY OF LAW tags from some furniture.

Unfortunately, Hofnagel, who does not have one of the best minds in science but does have great shoes, and Minoso, who is a terrific dancer, have never developed a model for testing the theory without actually removing one of those tags.

And right now, since no one really knows who puts them on furniture or what they mean, the risk to the universe as we know it is simply deemed too severe.

Still, Nemesis remains our greatest fear. How close to our solar system might it be? Maybe closer than we think. Some theorists believe it is only several hundred years behind the Comet Morty, which has already entered our solar system, much to the annoyance of everyone.

It has been called "a piece of junk" in America, "an overcooked schnitzel" in Germany, "a vile pellet from the mahsji lizard" in Indonesia, and an "I'm sorry, I think we have a bad connection" in Uruguay.

Although ninety-three miles in diameter, the Comet Morty passes quite near the earth, blinking amicably, and moves slowly enough to permit extended viewing. It is currently crawling across the skies of Sri Lanka, where it has lingered so long that people have started calling their elected officials and writing letters to the local newspapers, asking when it is going to be possible to get a decent night's sleep once again and why something can't be done to shoo it off.

Sri Lankan astrophysicists, most of whom have time-consuming day jobs, have thrown up their hands, and Jim at D'Onofrio's says he's not taking any more comets because parts are so hard to get and because "when all is said and done, I hardly make anything on comets."

Educating Roy
(or My Man Ate It)

I grew up on those Albert Payson Terhune books about collies who ran around performing knightly deeds.

In those days, I was not allowed to own a dog, so I was gulled into believing that these books actually contained reasonable representations of dog behavior.

I understand now that

1. Albert Payson Terhune was not allowed to own dogs either and was pretty much guessing about how they might act, or

2. The collies in his books were on drugs, or

3. Albert Payson Terhune was on drugs, or

4. Albert Payson Terhune was the pen name for a bunch of collies.

As a matter of fact, the collie lobby makes the NRA look like a bunch of milquetoasts. No sooner did they wash their paws of Terhune than they unleashed Lassie on us.

A bunch of us were talking about the television show "Lassie" one night, and several people in the group admitted that, as kids, they would burst into tears when the opening theme music came on and stay in a state of agitation for the whole show.

I knew exactly what they meant. As a kid, I could never understand the popularity of "Lassie." It made me nervous even to think about the show. Other homilists have noted that the humans who populated Lassie's world were a bunch of actuarial nightmares.

They couldn't head into town for a loaf of bread without getting caught in a crevasse or bitten by a rattlesnake. They inhabited a world—we would learn more about such places years later by watching "Star Trek"—in which the very marrow of the earth seemed impregnated with malice toward human life.

They were also dumb as pea turkeys. Lassie was the only one with a lick of sense, and after a while, she began to look like a tremendously harassed middle manager in a department full of goldbricks and nincompoops. Had the show gone on much longer, Lassie would probably have started developing all kinds of stress-related tics and gulping Mylanta tablets and wearing bifocals and scheduling more and more unexplained, prolonged absences from the farm.

As a child, I regarded life as an unreasonably terrifying proposition, even though my life was like a protracted stay in Michael Jackson's oxygen chamber, compared to life on "Lassie." I was not in the market for a more horrifying world view in which the only possible salvation was a knightly dog, which, as I said, I did not have.

Now that I am older, I find I can more or less live with life in all its abundant fearsomeness, but I cannot live with the idea that there are knightly dogs. I own a dog now, and I know him and his friends, and the only knight they resemble at all is Mordred.

My dog is Roy, a cross of German shepherd, wolverine, husky, Tasmanian devil, and perhaps some kind of pointer. He points, anyway. But not in a manner that suggests helpfulness. We obtained him from the Humane Society, where he had been left by his original owner, Satan, who could no longer manage him.

Roy's most notable features are his eyes, one bright blue and one brown flecked with blue. They enable him to achieve a wide variety of facial expressions, the most benign of which seems to ask, "So just how comprehensive is your homeowner's insurance?"

I began trying to train Roy out of a book called *How to Be Your Dog's Best Friend*, written by the Monks of New Skete, New York.

No kidding. There is a monastery in New Skete where the monks train German shepherds. The pictures made it look like a very appealing place, and I was drawn to idea of a monk-based dog-training technique because I felt I would, very soon, have to call on a Higher Power for help.

On the other hand, how much help can monks really be? They think it's easy to train dogs. Of course, they have the spiritual cards stacked in their favor, and they have gone to quite a bit of trouble to arrive at a state of tranquillity from which to begin.

The monks were very keen on having the dog owner establish him or herself as the "alpha" or lead wolf in his or her metaphorical pack. In other words, I was to persuade Roy and mayhaps also my wife that I was the alpha wolf and entitled to all the deference and perquisites that office entails. Seems like an unreasonable request. Roy has, after all, a running start on me at being a wolf. And then there's all the years I have put in trying to become a human being. Am I expected to veer suddenly off the trail of my life and pursue wolfhood?

The other big problem I faced was that I was not my dog's best friend, nor did I really want to be. Roy's best friend is (or, at least, was) Spanky, a black-and-white dog who lives down the street. Spanky began playing with Roy when Roy was a little puppy. Their game was slightly akin to bullfighting in that, when you felt you had vanquished your foe, you so indicated by biting his ear. (This is one of the many reasons I didn't want to be Roy's best friend.) As the months slid by, Roy got so he could keep Spanky on the ropes from the opening bell. In recent days, Spanky has taken on the mien of Muhammad Ali in the twilight of his ring career: confused, sullen, the lightning abruptly gone from his jab.

I watched Spanky's decline and feared a similar fate for myself. The monks, I had come to realize, could not help me, unless I decided to become one of them without notifying Roy. Just drive up to New Skete, take my vows, and spend my days in fervent prayer that Roy would never find me.

Basically, I think I would make an okay monk, if the order could see its way clear to cutting me some slack in one or two key areas, but I doubted it would (you make an exception for one guy, and then everybody is going to want to bring his wife), so I enrolled Roy in dog obedience classes.

The first thing Roy learned was that the term "dog obedience

classes" does not refer to classes in which humans are taught to
obey dogs. So he considered them a tremendous waste of his valuable time. He devoted himself instead to forming the first chapter
of SDS (Students for a Dog-dominated Society).

We owners attended the first night of classes without our dogs.
The teacher was a pleasant woman with an uncanny gift for sizing
up dogs. She told us that dogs never flunk her class. Only people
flunk. It was disturbingly clear whose side she was on. She concluded her talk with a little parable about Helen Keller and Annie
Sullivan. I believe it was intended to illustrate the value of breaking down barriers in communication. I realize it might seem offen-
sive to compare Helen Keller to an untrained dog, were it not for
the fact that the speaker clearly considered dogs to be far superior,
morally and spiritually, to people.

One exasperated-looking woman interrupted the orientation
session several times with nervous questions about her dog, who
was, I gathered, a terrible monster and who kept the entire household in a state of cowering submission. Her overall bearing was
not unlike that of Ellen Burstyn in *The Exorcist* when, haggard and
nerve-wracked, she finally goes to seek out an exorcist.

The woman showed up at class the following week with a little,
black, feckless dog whose downtrodden countenance was strongly
reminiscent of the sort of dog George Booth so often draws into
the scenery of his cartoons. The dog proved absurdly easy to train.

The teacher looked at Roy on his first night in class and said,
"He's immature for his age. You'll have to go very slowly to make
any progress with him." I told you she was uncanny.

I came to dread Monday nights. The problem in educating Roy,
I discovered, is that all dog-training commands are predicated on
the dog's starting from a more or less neutral position. The dog, in
theory, begins in a state of innocence (hah!). The task of the
trainer, in theory, is to make his oral commands understood and to
overcome the dog's "natural inclination," which is, in theory, to do
nothing at all. That, indeed, is the natural inclination of most dogs.

All of these theories, however, do not work as well when the
dog seizes the leash in its mouth, flops over on its back and com-
mences to do a Linda Blair impersonation, which is what Roy did

while the Ellen Burstyn lady's lobotomized dog marched around like the head of an ROTC class.

Our classes were held in the local YMCA gymnasium. The owners would move around in a large circle, urging their dogs in highstrung voices, while people sat on the sidelines in folding chairs and laughed their kneecaps off. I never did figure out who those people were. Maybe they come down to the YMCA most every night and just watch whatever is playing.

I would have laughed too, if I had not been playing such a huge role in the entertainment. As the weeks lapsed into months, I lapsed into a depression, because whenever I dared take my eyes off Roy and glance around the circle, the other dogs were all fulfilling the Helen Keller dream, going on to lead productive lives and win the admiration of presidents, while Roy and I remained trapped on page three of *The Miracle Worker.*

You will recall that only people flunk, so Roy, having served his hitch, was entitled to a diploma. I was down with the flu, possibly psychosomatic, on graduation night, so the fleaskin was mailed to us. I felt guilty for making Roy miss the pomp and circumstance, so I did a little yearbook write-up for him.

Here it is. (Sending this one out for Boz, Cookie, Max, Ingrid, Chelsea, Satin, and the whole gang down at Heeling High. It's been a great seven weeks. See you at the reunion. *Dawgeamus igitur.*)

ROY B. MC ENROE: Varsity Digging 3,4 . . . Squirrel Haters Club 2,3,4 . . . Dead mouse in Miss Hoolihan's locker . . . "I'd rather be chewing up valuable tapestries!" . . . The Who . . . Cruising for garbage . . . Ingrid

So Roy's golden academic days were behind him. He and I faced the future with little to aid us except the old rugged cross and such faith as we, soldiers of New Skete, could muster.

A few months after graduation, I read of a contest sponsored by the Ralston-Purina Company to choose the Great American Dog.

The winner gets $25,000 and a ride on the Purina float in the Macy's Thanksgiving Day Parade.

I considered entering Roy, mostly because the sum of $25,000 comes so close to covering the damage he has caused in my life that it seemed like kismet. I have been stopped short by several considerations, not the least of which is my feeling that the Macy's parade is not ready for him.

Roy would be sure to steal a sequined shoe from Miss Swiss Chard on the American Synod of Swiss Chard Producers Float right behind us, possibly after gnawing through the ropes which lashed the giant inflated stalk of leafy chard to its moorings. I have lived through enough of these episodes to know that, as I endeavored to apologize to Miss Swiss Chard, retrieve the shoe, and explain to the police officers that I simply must cross the security line because my dog has just run off with a satchel containing the $25,000 in his mouth, my foot would get tangled in one of the gnawed ropes in such a way that Miss Swiss Chard and I would ascend together into the November firmament until all that could be seen of us was a green, leafy speck against the slate-gray skies, and Phyllis George would be heard to extemporize, "Well, I guess that's the last we'll ever see of Colblain McIntosh," and for once, she would be pretty much right.

Roy would be seen in a subsequent episode of "60 Minutes," having donned sunglasses to hurry from his limo to the electronic gate of his posh Venezuelan retreat, after brusquely refusing to grant Diane Sawyer an interview about his tax situation.

Anyway, to enter this contest, I would have to write a fifty-word essay, from the dog's point of view, beginning with the words "I know I'm one of the family because . . ."

Because . . . because . . . because if I weren't, there would be extensive legal action pending against me.

It is a tremendous fallacy to suppose that Roy would even think in those terms. He would be more inclined to write, "I have decided to allow the two-legged infidels to share my life with me because . . ."

I don't mean to suggest that Roy dislikes us. Nothing could be further from the truth. It's the way he likes us that makes him perhaps inappropriate for the sort of poster dog Purina probably has in mind. For example, on two different occasions, Roy, while loitering outside, has been seized by a sudden desire to see me and/ or my wife, who has/have been loitering inside.

A Purina poster dog would come and scratch at the door. Roy simply raced, full tilt, at our aluminum storm door and crumpled its bottom panel like a piece of Reynolds Wrap. It was a little bit reminiscent of the way Superman used to barge in on crooks.

The first time it happened, I ordered a substitute panel and had it welded back into the frame. The second time it happened, I began to feel like a farmer in Alsace-Lorraine who continually repairs his fences and shacks only to have another marauding army sweep across the countryside.

We now have a storm door made of some kind of bazooka-tested titanium alloy. I give it about eighteen months.

Mostly, however, I have dealt with the situation by trying to be on the same side of the door as Roy. It means that I am outside a good deal more often than I would prefer, but it's a small price to pay for structural soundness.

I used to imagine naïvely that I could keep Roy outside on a chain. I looped the other end of his chain around one of the two metal poles which, as flying buttresses, supported our porch roof. That way, the chain could slide back and forth along the pole, which was bolted to the house in a way that I formerly regarded as impervious to canine exertions.

And so it was that one summer night, Roy was out on the porch, per his request, while my wife and I were in our living room, minding what we have to come to think of, somewhat defensively, as our own business.

When out on the porch there came such a clatter that I ran to the door. Our porch roof was swinging askew from the side of the house, wobbling in the night air on its one remaining buttress like a swiss chard float straining against the earthly shackle of a lone ungnawed guide rope.

Roy had become sufficiently interested in something to wrench the whole shebang out of its moorings. We didn't have to guess about what that something was, because the night air was filled with the odor of several thousand onions dropped into a vat of molten tires and doused liberally with condor urine. Roy himself was twisting around on his back on the ground the way World Cup soccer players do when they want the ref and the world to know how badly they have been fouled.

When I say that a skunk had sprayed our little corner of God's green earth, I am concerned that you will summon up a memory of skunk smells you have encountered driving along country roads at night, often when a skunk has recently joined the celestial petting zoo.

That is but a pale olfactory shadow of skunk fumes which are as fresh as today's headlines. And this skunk in particular must have been one of Schwarzeneggerian proportions on its way home from a bean and asparagus supper.

For that matter, could I just take this moment to say something about skunks? Unlike most animals, they get better press than they deserve. They are generally depicted—in cartoons and in science—as smelly but good-natured.

I don't buy it.

Few of its companions in the universe have quite such a definitive ace to play as does the skunk. And the skunk knows it. I know roughly what is going through a skunk's mind as it watches, say, a mixed-breed dog trailing a bit of porch-roof hardware, race toward it: "That's right. Keep coming. C'mon, c'mon. A little closer, right . . . THERE! Sucker! Hahahahahaha."

Like everybody else in the world, I carry around with me the not-entirely-convincing notion that tomato juice is somehow useful in counteracting skunk venom. So I washed Roy in it, and then I washed myself in it. Roy still smelled like a skunk victim, and I smelled like Campbell's Worst New Flavor. I repeated the process. The effect was to introduce an oh-so-subtle top-note of tomato into the essence of skunk which had impregnated the very stuff of our beings. Nothing less than an armada of fire-fighting helicopters swinging low for to drench our yard with all the Château Del Monte on the eastern seaboard was going to make a dent in our sorrows.

So we all went to bed smelly and got up smelly, but by then, blessed olfactory fatigue had descended on us, so that how we smelled was everybody else's problem.

I wondered what spiritual effect the episode would have on Roy.

When he is moved to articulate some deeply felt poetic insight stirring in his soul, Roy digs a hole. The perspicacious dog owner will develop the ability to see, in the contours, nooks, and furrows of a given hole, poetic conceits expressed as surely as if they were oxymorons and zeugmas, dactyls and spondees. I have honed my hole-appreciating sensibilities to a point where I am getting to be the Louis Untermeyer of holes.

The morning after the skunk attack, Roy dug a hole in which I thought I saw a touch of Hart Crane, although there was ridging and a use of severed roots which paid unmistakable homage to Eliot. I saw in the hole a keenly felt loss of innocence and a perception of polymorphous treachery.

There was, in the nuances of the hole, a revelation I had not considered—that the devilish animal had looked a good deal like the benighted Spanky. Roy may have regarded the whole incident as an atonement, of Old Testament proportions, for his past transgressions against Spanky.

He has been treating Spanky a little better lately, which hasn't solved any of my problems but which does provide me with some assurance that there is justice in the world.

But if the folks at the Ralston-Purina Company expect me to boil all these complexities down to fifty words, they have grossly overestimated my talents as an anthologist and dog owner. And that wouldn't be hard to do.

Stemming the Tide
with Dr. Plant

Even as I was writing this book, word got around, and we received a number of phone calls from folks who wondered if the book would deal at all with the plant world, particularly insofar as plants sometimes behaved like animals.

Unfortunately, interstate licensing problems—you folks in the Dakotas know especially, I think, what I mean—prevent me from fully speaking my mind on this subject.

Fortunately, I was able to reach Dr. Plant in his windblown mountain aerie, where, aided only by his purblind Sherpa Noh and a cockapoo named Desiree, he wrestles with the darkest questions of the houseplant world.

Dr. Plant has graciously agreed to share some of his most fascinating case histories. Do not ask me where he can be reached. That must remain a secret, since there is a price, if that is the right word, on his head among the plants. Correspondences sent to me will be forwarded.

Here now are the stories of others who have written, seeking his aid.

DEAR DR. PLANT: Last night my Horrificus viperius slithered out of its pot, opened the refrigerator, ate two Dell Monica (sp?) steaks, drank a bottle of Grand Marnier, smashed all of my husband's Django Reinhardt records, set off the burglar alarm, and tore the stuffing out of our throw pillows. We're frightened to leave our bedroom now, and the plant has its coils around our beloved cat, a black Angora with one white paw named Ernie. What can we do? Answer quick.

Mrs. Opah, Kalamazoo, Michigan

DEAR MRS. OPAH: The Horrificus is a moody, suspicious plant which may read a good deal more into your behavior than is really there. Dr. Plant advises less sandy soil, a tad more water, and a countenance of utter impassivity. Also, Dr. Plant does not write a pet column, but he cannot but wonder if your practice of naming your cat's feet has occasioned some jealousy on the part of the Horrificus.

DEAR DR. PLANT: Despite loving care and great personal sacrifice on my part, my $150 Durwoodus kirbiferus orchid is brown and dry. Bits of it crumble into dust at the slightest touch. Also, it lies in a heap instead of standing up in the pot. What is this condition called?

Darby Skink, Tallahassee, Florida

DEAR MR. SKINK: Death.

DEAR DR. PLANT: Last night, I came home early from bowling and caught my husband fondling the leaves of our Gurgling Red Spindle and cooing terms of endearment. He claims he was only checking for cuddlebugs, which is one of the terms I heard him coo. Is there any such thing? Also, do you think my husband is, like, a pervert or a closet homosexual?

Erma Gomp, Boca Raton, Florida

DEAR MRS. GOMP: That would depend on whether he was touching the pistil or the stamen. To speak to the other matter, there is no such thing as a cuddlebug. On the other hand, Dr. Plant has often thought that the Purple Woolly Mite, which attacks the Red Spindle, has a soft, huggable quality.

DEAR DR. PLANT: Recently I bought five Alpaca Virus Ferns. Do I water them every day?

Moira Carma, Pine Barrens, New Jersey

DEAR MS. CARMA: How is Dr. Plant supposed to know whether you water them every day or not? Dr. Plant does not live with you, nor does he want to. Dr. Plant has chosen a noble but lonely course for his life and feels no regret. If you are all that curious, perhaps you should ask a loved one to observe you closely for a period of several days to determine your watering habits.

DEAR DR. PLANT: Recently I sent away for an Uruguayan Whooping Fig plant I saw advertised in a magazine. When it arrived, it had gray furry mold all over it and only two droopy leaves. That is not the way I had pictured it looking at all. Can I get my money back? P.S. It has not produced any figs per se, and it is starting to smell like the dickens.

Ralph Meany, Decatur, Illinois

DEAR MR. MEANY: Your "plant" is a dead rabbit. The Uruguayan government has been running this scam for years as a way of getting rid of its many dead rabbits and turning a tidy profit in the bargain. I doubt you can get your money back, but do not overlook the possibility of salvaging a pair of fig-lined gloves out of the deal.

DEAR DR. PLANT: Recently our Deploring Jade began to sulk. Then we saw big red spiders on it. Then, last night, one of them jumped off and bit Grandmother on the nose. You know, she got upset and pureed that sucker in the GE food processor. The same thing happened an hour later, but there was tomorrow's wort slaw in the GE at the moment. Well, it was tomorrow's, but now nobody will eat it. What do you advise?

Bertram Og, Chagrin Falls, Ohio

DEAR MR. OG: About the plant, your grandmother, the leftover slaw, or your family's peculiar eating habits? Dr. Plant's inclination is to use your grandmother's nose to lure the spiders off the Jade, but that may not fit your situation.

DEAR DR. PLANT: When I trim my succulents, the lush umbrels go droopy. Also, my clivias are pining. What should I do?

Agnes Wrench, Texarkana, Texas

DEAR Ms. WRENCH: Are you sure this is a plant question?

Is It Okay to Crow "Duck" in a Crowded Dovecote?

My grandmother practiced pigeon birth control.

She lived over the sort of small grocery store that is harder and harder to find in America nowadays. A sign announcing the grocery store's presence ran across the front of the building, just below my grandmother's windows. The pigeons in town had adopted it as their own personal Capistrano. There was a cozy area behind the sign. The pigeons thought it was just great for multifamily housing.

My grandmother loved animals, but she seemed to think there were enough pigeons in the world. She never explained how she arrived at that determination, and I, her loyal sidekick, never asked. Her birth-control program involved waiting until the pigeons were on whatever sort of errands pigeons do, leaning out the window, and removing such eggs as had been laid behind the sign.

My grandmother hoped the pigeons would sense a certain strain of futility creeping into their lives and go elsewhere.

A lot she knew. If pigeons have not yet come to perceive their lives as futile, it would take a great deal more than the theft of a few eggs to call futility to their attention.

Anyway, the pigeons didn't leave. They were fruitful and multiplied. I believe this is because pigeons are produced in some other way. The eggs, I think, are just a decoy. My fantasy is that full-grown pigeons stream constantly, in a blurred procession, up out of a hole in the ground near Lincoln, Nebraska, and fly to their assigned destinations around the world. Nobody knows how pigeons are made. There are no baby pigeons. Have you ever seen a baby pigeon? Well, then.

That was many years ago. In these disputatious times, my grandmother would have been slapped with an injunction by some pigeon's-rights legal-aid group. That is the subject of this essay: Birds and the Law. We will attempt to treat the subject with the dignity and aplomb it requires of us.

Now, let us first turn our gaze upon sunny Columbus, Ohio, where the general state of merriment and good cheer is broken only by the occasional flaming bird.

No, strike that remark. That is the kind of thing we are trying to avoid. Not an hour ago, a woman called me at this newspaper where I work and told me I was sensationalistic and tawdry and ignorant. And it was not my wife. I mean to shake that reputation and prove to you that I do not need to stoop to a flaming bird to hold your attention.

Let us begin again by looking at this Columbus case in another way. Ahem. There are few areas in which the nobility of our human spirit breaks down so infamously as it does in the area of the Security Deposit. Landlords and tenants—each anticipating heinous behavior from the other—try to get the jump on each other in nastiness. True?

We would all do well to consider what Rousseau says about security deposits in his *Social Contract*—which is nothing. Philosophers have, in general, wimped out on this subject, because they don't care to gaze directly into this sucking wound of human malevolence.

Why, the very name itself is misleading. From the word go, neither party feels any too secure about the deposit. (I think we're losing them, best bring out that flaming bird.) A recent court case in Columbus, Ohio—prefigured by the appearance of a flaming bird—illustrates exactly what I am getting at.

Robert and Cathy Gessler won a decision against their landlord, who had confiscated their security deposit of $425. One of the disputed items was a burn on the carpet. The landlord blamed the

Gesslers for allowing the fireplace embers to escape. The Gesslers
claimed that a flaming bird had bounced out of the fireplace.

The UPI wire-service story (and they call *me* sensationalistic)
said the bird "dived kamikaze-style through a chimney into a fireplace and landed dead on the living room carpet of a rented
house."

Lawrence Charles Gaba, attorney for the Gesslers, could not
confirm this version when I reached him by telephone. Gaba said
the bird was up on the chimney, asphyxiated on the smoke, fell
down the chimney, and came to its more or less final resting place
on the carpet.

"My stars, this is a grisly tale," I blurted.

"It could have been worse," Lawrence Charles Gaba responded
equably. I did not inquire as to what he meant. Lawyers have particularly lurid imaginations.

It should be added that Gaba was nonplussed, in a pleasant way,
about all the attention his case was getting. He reflected that he
had led a long and distinguished legal career, defended murderers,
etc., and was now teetering on the edge of an unwholesome sort of
fame thanks to the efforts of a flaming bird.

Anyway, the UPI version of the case, in which the bird seemed
almost to be making some kind of statement about the futility of
life (perhaps for the benefit of pigeons), did not hold up.

I asked Gaba if he had called any witnesses to back up the
Gesslers' version of what happened. No, he said, but since their
story was not contradicted by the opposition, it enjoyed, in his
view, the legal standing of truth.

I'm not sure how the opposition would have gone about contra-
dicting the story. I suppose the landlord could have brought in a
few expert witnesses, but how many certified pyro-ornithologists
can the Greater Columbus area be expected to cough up?

Obviously, it is difficult to think about the Gaba case without a
growing knot of sadness in one's heart for the bird. Gaba, who
viewed the bird as a very secondary issue, took pains to get me to
see the broader principles at work in the case. I believe he fancied
it a triumph of Buckeye populism.

He may have been underselling it.

The court apparently decided it was not the Gesslers' duty to anticipate the bird's arrival (the legal principle here being, I believe, *avis ex machina*). The flaming bird would therefore fall into the category sometimes known as "acts of God." The enlightened reader certainly will not have failed to note the echoes of the phoenix myth present in the story.

The phoenix, a flaming bird, recurs in a surprising number of mythologies and religions, usually as a symbol of immortality. The ancient Chinese believed the appearance of a phoenix preceded a momentous event of some kind. The ancient Chinese, however, often went a lot longer between momentous events than we do now. These are tumultuous times. We rarely go more than a day or two without a momentous event, so hooking each one up with the right flaming bird is durn near impossible.

The Columbus court, at least, was big enough to admit it could not adjudicate the behavior of birds. Would that all of our solons practiced such restraint.

In Connecticut, where I live, we recently came within a feather's breadth of right-to-peck legislation. I speak of course of the late, unlamented Schmidle Act.

In 1985, State Representative Mae S. Schmidle, a Newtown, Connecticut, Republican, took it upon herself to propose legislation which would have banned the throwing of uncooked rice at weddings.

Representative Schmidle (whose name is, I believe, pronounced just the way a Jewish tailor might say, in a dismissing fashion, "middle, schmiddle") believed that the rice was being eaten by birds who could not digest it and would sometimes die.

And I thought the Republicans were going to get Big Government off all of our backs.

Frankly, I could never imagine how this law would work. Would a paddy wagon pull up to the steps of the chapel?

"Ladies and gentlemen, drop your rice and come out with your hands up. You're under arrest for violation of the Schmidle Act."

"Even Uncle Max?"

"Book 'em, Dan-o."

I found myself getting paranoid while the debate raged over the

Schmidle bill. I was watching a downy woodpecker go at some suet on my bird feeder one morning. Jeez, I thought, he's really eating a lot of it. What if he gets sick? What if he has a heart attack from all that suet? Would it be my fault? Would I be *liable?*

I mean, normally I kind of expect the birds to use good judgment.

Meanwhile, the press began tracking down experts who doubted that birds were in any danger from eating wedding rice.

A biology professor at the University of Connecticut was quoted thusly: "The only way rice could hurt a bird at a wedding is if you hit it right in the face with it."

A former Connecticut Audubon Society official speculated to one reporter that rice might kill birds "if you dropped a ten-pound sack on their heads."

It was not clear from the news stories whether these guys were debating the merits of the bill or discussing creative ways to kill birds with rice. (Is it possible that people who devote their careers to the examination and protection of birds eventually wind up choking back hostility toward them?)

Personally, I prefer filing a single kernel of rice to pinpoint sharpness, dipping it in curare, fastening it to an umbrella tip, and sneaking up behind the bird at a crowded intersection. It's neater, and it gives me something to do with my hands.

When the whole flap over the Schmidle bill started, I had a notion that the rice was dangerous because the birds would eat it and then drink a whole lot of water, causing the rice to expand in their stomachs.

I see now that, if this were true, birds would spontaneously explode from time to time, especially in June. You would be walking BLAM! down a sunny street and BLAM! birds BLAM! would blow up as you passed.

But they don't.

Well, the bill did not pass, but I suppose it may come around again. If it ever passed, I guess I would not miss throwing rice. The ancient Hindus started that tradition at weddings, as a symbolic bestowing of fecundity (which they now need the way they need more cobras). The Hindus, however, had the decency not to sling the rice around like a bunch of bleacher bums. Their bride and groom would each gently pour three handfuls of it over the other. The overhand Uncle Ben fastball is a typically Western bit of boobery.

So if we ever do legislate against rice, we should, in the same law, also legislate underhanded tossing of whatever is tossed.

Whatever indeed.

I have made an investigation of possible substitutes for uncooked rice. Here are some ideas:

1. Cooked rice. It would feel gross. Fresh cooked rice might burn, and cooked rice that's been sitting around tends to glob up.

2. Birdseed. This is not unheard of, even in these unschmidled times. I know a real-life, actual bride who was pelted with birdseed at her wedding, and she hated it. She claimed it got in her underwear. Wedding nights, in this essayist's opinion, are tricky enough as it is.

3. Couscous. Still awaiting FDA approval for wedding use.

4. Gravel. Not classy enough.

5. Fits. I'm sure we have all been at weddings where these have been thrown.

6. Leftover Halloween candy corn. This is an appealing thought, because it would solve the unrelated problem of what to do with leftover Halloween candy corn, which nobody likes and which must be stored in huge vats in North Dakota until someone can think of a safe alternative.

In test throws, however, the candy corn tends to yaw through the air in a way that could be hazardous to the wedding couple.

For now, anyway, we all breathe a sigh of relief at the Schmidle bill's demise . . . perhaps followed by an admiring inhalation for a lawmaker with some vision and, well, pluck.

In fact, I went so far as to write a new Schmidle campaign song, to be sung to "Diamonds Are a Girl's Best Friend."

I offer it here, for the first time on any page:

A peck at a worm may be quite unsuccessful,
But Schmidle is a bird's best friend.
And rice may be grand, but it won't feed the nestful

In your humble tree, so go bite Tippi Hedren's knee.
Peewees flee and finches flinch
And we all feel the pinch in the end.
But hawk, dove, or kestrel,
That rice don't digest well,
And Schmidle is a bird's best friend!

The End

Implacable You:
Bigfoot Has Lunch
with a Short-Story Writer

"Do you know me? Most people have heard of me, but I'm not always recognized. That's why I carry this," says Bigfoot, holding up a small piece of green plastic. He is showing me the way he would do an American Express commercial. "What do you think?" he asks me anxiously.

"I think you shouldn't bare your teeth so much," I tell him.

"Mr. T does," says Bigfoot.

"Mr. T's teeth aren't five inches long and pointy," I tell him.

"American Express, because you never know when you'll have to put your big foot down," Bigfoot muses. "American Express, because . . . because you're not that famous yeti . . . because life can be so abominable . . . because people might give you sass, quatch."

"Yuck," I say. Bigfoot and I are having lunch in a restaurant neither one of us can remember having recommended to the other.

"I see you doing maybe one of those commercials for a plaque-fighting toothpaste," I tell him.

"What is plaque?" Bigfoot asks.

"Plaque is the new frontier of self," I answer. "They're sounding the clarion call to battle already. In the next few years, we are going to fight plaque the way we fought B.O., dragon breath, foot sweat, body fat, and sundry personal gases."

"And it's on your teeth?" says Bigfoot.

"It's everywhere," I muse. "It's a vague medical term for imperfectly understood substances which accumulate on various planes and surfaces of the body, as if microorganisms were Jaycees who could not stay anywhere for very long without nailing up a tablet to commemorate their presence."

Bigfoot looks dumbfounded.

Outside I can see the cars spill across the arc of the freeway in an unbroken chrome snake, and I want to pick up the rubber troll and the little click-clack device of metal balls and string and wood and the baseball cap with the fake soft-sculpture horns, pick them all up, all the symbols cluttering our table and this story, pick them up and stumble out into the slate afternoon, get in the Nissan and drive somewhere.

"Let's go somewhere, drive aimlessly, I don't know, the mall," I say.

"What's a mall?" says Bigfoot, and for a moment he looks to me like David Hartman, the "Good Morning, America" guy, except Bigfoot's hairline is receding. He is apelike and yet not apelike.

"A mall is . . ." I say, and then give up.

"This is good," Bigfoot exclaims, spooning up another and then another mouthful of chilled melon and champagne soup. "I never heard of this before. You know, sometimes I feel as though life is passing me by. Wandering around in the woods, skulking in swamps, hiking in the mountains once in a while. I think the last movie I saw was *Dr. Zhivago.* And since the wife and I split up, I don't fuss very much with food—just do whatever's the easiest. If I'm hungry I catch a squirrel and eat it in front of the TV or something. Or Lean Cuisine. I've tried that a couple of times."

He has talked too long, and Bigfoot knows it. He blushes and falls silent. A waiter hovers solicitously nearby. Dressed in a tan poplin suit, pinstriped shirt, and knit tie, Bigfoot attracts very little notice here, except when he accidentally starts to eat a wicker basket.

"Let's get out of here," I say, and we leave.

We drive across town to where Deirdre is staying with an anarcho-Zen conceptual punk artist known as The Thing and Arpad Gotelantrodi, the Chadian nitro-violinist.

All three are in the back, by the pool. Bigfoot and I borrow trunks—does he need trunks? is he man, monster, mammoth, myth? I have no freaking idea—and dive in. The pool is bright azure, and for moments, I have angelic delusions of whirling through a liquid firmament, but then something snaps, and I am just disaffected.

Drying off, I listen to The Thing and Gotelantrodi arguing about music.

"So I believe if you assign a numerical value to every note to 'How Much Is That Doggie in the Window?' you can actually calculate how much the doggie costs," The Thing is saying. "Assuming you're into notes. I reject notes. Notes are worthless, outmoded garbage ways of looking at music."

"Alakandola bemoandatu doggiedoggie goba!" answers Gotelantrodi.

"Doesn't he speak English?" I whisper to Deirdre.

"I'm not even sure he speaks Chadian. Mostly he just plays the viola and blows up things," she answers.

"He's cool. If it's loud, it's cool," says The Thing.

"Who are you people?" asks Bigfoot, looking a bit frightened.

"I am The Thing. I am, in my personhood, that quality of being constituted as a thing. I am that which is thingness," says The Thing.

"What do you do?" asks Bigfoot.

"I'm in my omega-minimalist period. I don't do anything."

Bigfoot is looking more confused and frightened by the minute, and I kind of want him to bolt into the mountains and never be seen again, but I kind of don't, also. So we split and go back to my apartment.

We try to watch television in my apartment, but my television set has some kind of worsening organic syndrome that causes Mary Lou Retton to crop up on the screen, so that after you have been watching it for a while, there are nothing but Mary Lou Rettons on the air—productions of *Hamlet* and *Death of a Salesman* and "Hill Street Blues" populated entirely by soaring, leaping Mary Lou Rettons doing reverse hechts and twisting tsukaharas during their soliloquies.

We watch Mary Lou do the "Charlie, you was my brother . . ." speech on the parallel bars until we can't stand it. We switch channels, and there she is, hosting a telethon to raise money to fight . . . plaque.

"Well, there goes that," says Bigfoot. He heaves himself out of the Swedish kneeling chair, and suddenly, he is more apelike than I remember. He walks out the door and slowly up the street, headed out of town.

I want to stop him, keep him here, but I don't get up. I feel plaque, as a natural process, shifting over our bodies, ourselves, like tide-swept sand. I feel bowed by the weight of the world, but I know it is plaque, bearing down invisibly on the very core of my being.

The thing is, I don't care.

Carp, Carp, Carp

Although a skirted fish is, even in the abstract, a fearsome prospect, I would just as soon skirt fish, as a subject, altogether in this book, but for the possibility that I would be asked at some later date, "What about fish?"

Walking down a busy city street, how could I be jaunty-jolly, never knowing if the very next passerby might be the one to stop, stare coldly, and say, "What about fish, Kenneth?" Or someone might shout it out during the ceremony consecrating me as Metabishop of the First Worldwide Enzymatic Church of the Seed-in-the-Spirit. Not that I am in line for such a post right now. Not that I am even sure such a post exists. I just don't want "What about fish?" hanging over me. Don't want fish hanging over me in any way, shape, or form, actually.

All of which suggests that I suffer from Fish Anxiety. And so I do. In multiple forms.

First off, there is anxiety about fishing, that is to say angling. And then there is anxiety about having fish in a bowl around the house. Plus the anxiety the fish may feel.

I don't fish much, because I don't know how. The closest I ordinarily come to fishing is at a local supermarket where they have a tank of trout swimming around and looking, as trout do, more or less like Milton Berle. You don't fish for the trout so much as you point at one and, like a Roman Emperor, designate it for death.

I find I cannot do this, cannot turn my thumb down on a trout. It's not that I like Milton Berle so much. I just fear that I might look at the trout and see understanding—doomed understanding—in its eye.

My father, I believe, fished at some point in his life. At least, he had a number of largely inoperable reels moldering in our basement for the duration of my childhood. He also had several boxes of exotic-looking tackle. He and I would sometimes wander down there after dinner, open the boxes, and look at all that stuff, mostly to admire its enormous destructive potential, should it ever fall into the wrong hands.

The only time I actually went fishing—in the sense of standing near an allegedly fish-supporting body of water and attempting to withdraw live fish from it—with my father was one night on Cape Cod, in the company of my father's friend Bill Dougherty, a person of doleful countenance. We sat in the cold on a jetty for a long time and then left without catching anything.

I gathered, from the rather forlorn drift of the conversation, that people rarely caught anything while fishing and that the long strings of fish one sometimes saw dangling from the arms of beaming fishermen were acquired through some bleak and unsavory form of subterfuge.

So I was pretty surprised the next time I fished, many years later on a lake in Canada, to catch a pike. The fish seemed pretty surprised too, and Lord knows our fishing guide, Chet, was surprised because he had pretty much decided, in the course of the day, that I was the most useless person in North America. I could tell he was surprised by the way he said "Eh," which was the main thing he said to me all day, although not usually with such brio and verve. The only comparable "Eh" of the day came somewhat later when a snake swam up and tried to get into our boat.

Probably I shouldn't let that statement pass. A rather large snake did indeed swim right up to the boat and attempt to come aboard. It looked to me—I am not a herpetologist, but I play one on television—like an ordinarily land-based snake. That is, a snake which ordinarily conducts its affairs on land. My current theory is that the snake was tired of swimming and wanted to rest. That is a theory I have worked up over the course of many contemplative nights in my armchair by the fireside. My only theory right at that time was that the snake should in no wise be allowed in the boat. This is an area where Chet and I were in total agreement, and we lashed recklessly at the reptile with our fishing poles until my wife suggested that the snake might actually slither right up one of our poles and into the boat.

Whereupon Chet and I stopped lashing and looked mutely at each other while the snake continued rearing and hissing, and I was dimly aware that Curt Gowdy had not, on any episode of "American Sportsman," prepared me for anything like this. On the other hand, the snake didn't look any too prepared either.

The whole incident put me (and possibly Chet) off fishing for a while.

What I do instead is attend fishing trade shows. I like to browse among the booths—which boast such colorful names as Morty the Knife Man and (I kid you not) S&M Flytying ("We have zonker strips" read a hand-lettered sign there)—and listen to the chatter of fishermen, which is gibberish.

"You goin' for fluke or crappies?"

"Jigs and teasers."

"You chummin' or giggin'?"

"Prolly use a shovelnose bucktail or peau de soie grommets."

This talk is anxiety-provoking enough, but at a recent Hartford Fishing Expo, I overheard a guy in one booth say, "Well, we just wanna set you up with the right transducer."

Wha'?

Meet the electronic angler. For years, it seems, fish have enjoyed the unfair advantage of being underwater, where they cannot be espied. Today's properly equipped fisherman has a little sonar screen on the poop deck to keep tabs on the turbot.

I struck up a conversation with a purveyor of fish surveillance systems, one Russ Watson. I asked Russ if he did not agree that multicolored state-of-the-art computer digital light-emitting-diode Starfish Wars gadgetry takes a wee bit of the mystery out of fishing, from the human perspective. (To the fish, wondering where Uncle Bernie went in such a gosh-darned hurry, the mystery continues.)

"I've used all this stuff and still got skunked," countered Russ, apparently unaware that this was not a dynamic sales pitch. "It's good for people like myself who have a limited amount of time to go fishing and want to maximize that time."

I dunno. Sounds kind of Type A to me. Sonar probably ought to be restricted to leaning out over the gunwale from time to time and saying "Eh" at the water. You go fishing to forget your worries. Then you worry you won't catch fish before you have to go back to your worries. So you drop a few grand on sonar. Then you worry that it won't work or that it will work too well. It's a vertiginous spiral of Fish Anxiety.

Which brings us to the fish in the bowl. I read a report in 1984 of a study, done in Wales, which concluded that goldfish swimming alone in bowls may be anxious. Of course, everybody in Wales may be anxious. They all certainly look a little anxious. Actually, Richard Burton looked like certain goldfish. And vice versa. I don't know if the study had any particular ramifications in Wales. Maybe people started throwing the occasional shot of brandy into their goldfish bowls.

The Welsh scientists studied "feral" goldfish. This is an interesting term. Kind of has a Jack London ring to it. *Orville—Wild Goldfish of the Yukon.* The term actually refers to goldfish who have been turned loose in ponds and streams. Goldfish who are not looking for a handout from anyone, who are making it on their own. Which brings up an interesting side of Fish Anxiety.

In order to explore it, however, I think we will need a short historical overview of goldfish.

A SHORT HISTORICAL OVERVIEW OF GOLDFISH

Ahem.

The Chinese first bred goldfish some thousand years ago. They (goldfish) belong in the category (which also takes in Ming vases and fireworks) of Things People Did to Keep from Getting Bored in China.

The most important person to protect from boredom was the Emperor. If the Emperor grew bored, he might think up a rainy-day project for everyone to do, like building an enormous wall across one side of the country. Consequently, many people were engaged in keeping things lively for him.

It is a safe guess that it was one of these people who began selectively breeding a species of unattractive, brownish, carplike fish. The fish had such a feckless attitude toward its own gene structure that it was really no trouble at all to persuade it, over the course of a few generations, to become bright and shiny and orange.

This worked out just great. The fish looked absolutely socko, and the Emperor was so entertained by it that it never occurred to him to have everybody, for instance, put aluminum siding on the wall or build a roof over the entire country.

And even unto this day, all over Asia, goldfish are revered, prized, and carefully bred. People look at them and are just knocked out and walk around all the doo-dah day smiling and becoming economically superior to us.

Then Western civilization got hold of the goldfish, and it took about seventeen minutes before somebody decided to start mass-breeding them so that every single kid in America could have a little bowl with a goldfish swimming around in it.

This accomplished three things:

1. Every kid got a goldfish.
2. Goldfish started looking more and more like their unattractive, scavenging, carplike forebears (or in this case, forefish) because of indiscriminate breeding.
3. People started growing up with Goldfish Anxiety.

Ladies and gentlemen, I thank you.

END OF THE SHORT HISTORICAL OVERVIEW (There will be a brief intermission, during which you may put the book down, get up, stretch your legs, and greet your neighbors.)

Welcome back.

What do I mean by Goldfish Anxiety? I think you know what I mean, mister. No point in playing dumb with me.

You have sat there in a room with a goldfish and found your eye straying toward the bowl. Questions bubble up in your brain. You start thinking all kinds of stuff. It really opens up a can of worms.

Is the goldfish bored? Does it know where it is? Does it understand that there is no water out here? Does the goldfish have any greater expectations? Does it comprehend its own mortality? If you are unlucky, right about the time you start contemplating this last question, the goldfish will demonstrate that it comprehends its mortality more fully than you do. It will die.

(A personal existentialist underview: Some friends of mine once named a goldfish Colin, because I won it for them at a fair by throwing a Ping-Pong ball into its bowl. They put the goldfish in a little pond by their patio to eat mosquitoes. I called them up a week later and inquired jovially, "So, how am 'I' doing?" "You're dead," they replied. "A raccoon ate you." You think Kierkegaard ever had to put up with that?)

The way people deal with their goldfish anxiety is to turn their goldfish loose in streams and ponds. The scientists in Wales discovered that the goldfish, thus freed, naturally form schools, which made the scientists think goldfish are naturally gregarious and thus anxious when kept alone in a bowl.

Goldfish are also naturally imperialistic. They eat the babies of other kinds of fish. They turn their aquatic environments into giant carposystems.

Do you see what I'm getting at? I don't want to push any panic buttons, but I think if the current trends in Goldfish Anxiety continue, we are going to be sorry, a few years down the road, that nobody in China knew how to juggle.

STUDY QUESTIONS

(Using the end of your pencil, break the paper seal and open the examination booklet. You may begin.)

1. How did they order fish in ancient Rome?
2. Welsh mythology contains extensive references to Morty the Knife Man. Who is he?
3. What is the significance, among Japanese fish breeders, of the term "absolutely socko"?
4. Based on your reading of the above, the soundest conclusion you could draw is:

(a) Snakes should wear life preservers.

(b) Kierkegaard was a fish.

(c) Fish are trying to take over.

(d) Peau de soie makes an excellent lure.

5. What kind of hats, would you guess, do they wear in Wales?

You, Your Yard, and You Again

It's fairly tough to maintain a good relationship with the animals in your yard.

When I moved into my current house, for example, I put up bird feeders, figuring I would get the birds on my side right off the bat. That was before I knew that my yard was controlled by a vicious gang of squirrels the size of Rottweilers. While I watched, daunted and helpless, from the (relative) safety of my kitchen window, these squirrels leaped, like furry Flying Wallendas, from the trees and onto my bird feeders and commenced to actually crunch holes in the plastic with their teeth until they had reduced all my bird feeders to smithereens. No kidding. Squirrels did this.

So I ventured out the door and said, falteringly, "Uh, could we please have some, you know, order out here?"

The squirrels just gnashed their teeth at me and continued kicking disconsolately through the rubble, and I had a terrible feeling I was losing face with all the snakes and crows and raccoons and platypuses I knew to be lurking in the underbrush, gauging the mettle of the new administration.

I was right. The local Raccoon Commando Unit ("It's Not Just a Species, It's an Adventure") sized me up as a chump right away and began a series of nightly raids on my hapless garbage cans, under the generalship of a raccoon I pictured along the lines of

Robert Duvall in *Apocalypse Now:* "I love the smell of watermelon rinds at three in the morning!"

Sometimes, reviewing the carnage the following day, I had a hard time figuring out what had been eaten. Not that I keep any kind of strict inventory on my garbage, mind you. It just seemed that a lot of food had been passed over. It's possible that the raccoons are merely interested in keeping their skills sharp.

So we started "trading up" in garbage cans. We got all the way up to the metal kind with the elasticized cord that runs over the top and hooks onto the side handles. The raccoons had a little trouble with this, so they brought in a raccoon named Louie "Fingers" Almafitano, a garbage-can cracker out of Chicago. He had those suckers open and moldy cheesecake all over the driveway inside of five minutes.

I've held off so far on getting one of the new generation of "smart" garbage cans—the kind programmed to take evasive action or fire death rays at interlopers—until they get the bugs worked out.

Instead, the garbage debacle got me interested in the earthworms in my yard. Earthworms eat garbage, but in a fashion that is both less selective and less disruptive than the way of raccoons. In fact, the town in which I live, Avon, Connecticut, is running out of places to put its garbage, so the town fathers have been giving some thought to bringing in a whole bunch of earthworms to eat the garbage and turn it into fertile worm manure, which has its uses, I guess.

Earthworms have been figurative sugarplums dancing in the heads of benighted landfill engineers ever since the 1970s, when a federal study proved they would, under the right circumstances, eat a heap o' garbage.

The notion of bringing them to Avon was introduced by one of its citizens, one Edward J. Salliant, who farms worms and sells their manure as a hobby. During a debate on the matter, Salliant was quoted in the press as professing, "My business is not worm poop. It's financial planning." I cannot think of another person who has resolved so neatly in his own lifetime the question of what to chisel on his gravestone.

The town fathers of Avon, however, have not so far embraced the earthworms (definitely a one-sided proposition) as a concept. I suspect this is due, in part, to Avon's overall image as (despite the regrettable presence of a few homes like mine) a posh suburb. Many people who move to Avon have gone to some trouble to put a lot of distance between themselves and such considerations as worms, garbage, and fertile manure.

The town fathers must have asked themselves: What if it works? What if it's a howling success? That would be the worst. It could really put Avon on the map.

Avon is already on most maps, but it's conceivable that, on the sort of maps that feature little pictures of local attractions, the town would be marked by a worm eating a grapefruit rind.

Then you'd get tourists passing through:

" 'Scuse me. Which way to them nahtcorlers?"

"What?"

"Them nahtcorlers. Ones what eat waste."

Local establishments would start selling bumper stickers: "I'd rather be wiggling in Avon" or "This car climbed the Avon worm garbage heap." Lord, Lord.

And you'd get friends in other places hitting you up for bags of the fertilizer:

"Long as you and Mabel and the kids are driving down, any chance you could load in a bag of that worm guano for my geraniums?"

Actually, it's not even called anything as fashionable as "guano." Worm excrement is called "castings" for some reason. Certainly, nothing could be further from a worm's nature than to cast. "Castings" has kind of a P.R. ring, as though some copywriter was trying to distract us—and possibly the worms too—from the obvious drawbacks of armlessness.

The great worm debate, however, caused many of us Avonites to think a little bit harder about worms than is our ordinary wont. What are worms anyway? I was inclined to think they were insects, but I gather they're not. They hang around with insects, but they're something else.

I asked around, and it turns out that the one thing almost everybody knows for sure about worms is that they have sex with themselves. One individual worm, I mean, will have sex with him- or herself. Never mind. It's not true, anyway. If you are sitting around a bar discussing earthworms, it's something most people there will be sure to know, but it's actually a worm myth. Although an individual worm does have the sex organs of both genders, it still takes two worms to tango.

Speaking of which, the way earthworms move resembles, slightly, a tango. They spread their front parts forward and then squinch (I apologize for getting into some pretty technical language here) their back parts up to where the front parts have got to. And so on.

Armed with that kind of detailed scientific knowledge about worms, I began to look at my own personal backyard ecosystem in a whole new way. I was sitting (not literally) on about an acre of worms. If I could whip my earthworm herd into garbage-eating fettle, I might be able to thwart the marauding raccoon horde and feed my roses, which have never looked as healthy as the worms, the raccoons, or the garbage.

Like others before me, I began to see worms as a panacea. Until I found out there are a few qualifying aspects to the—you should pardon the expression—diet of worms.

Worms will eat up garbage insofar as it is stuff like blueberry cobbler, kohlrabi scraps, kiwi custard, etc. Worms will not eat a broken hat rack. Or an old toaster. Worms might not even eat a used Christmas tree. Maybe if you chopped it up for them and sprinkled some Parmesan cheese on it . . .

But that's another thing. It turns out you can't just throw a bunch of Twinkies and cantaloupes and Count Chocula cereal on the heap and expect the worms to tuck in. You have to grind it up first and mix it with some manure and . . . pretty soon you get to wondering just whose interests are being served here. I mean is this more of a landfill or a giant worm restaurant? That very kind of issue is what breeds unrest. You get folks grumbling, "If they treated us half as good as they treat them worms . . ."

And, in sooth, there came word from Ogden, Utah, where the worm-powered landfill concept had been tried, that worms are not

the bowl of cherries the Edward Salliants of this world might have
us believe them to be. A man named Cal Hubble, manager of the
Ogden landfill, was quoted thusly in the press: "I don't want to
hear any more about worms."

Which was fine, because there didn't seem to be anything anyone could tell Hubble about worms. He had employed them for
nine months and found them to be a bunch of shiftless, no-account
animals who, if they had shoulders, would put chips on them.

In particular, Hubble complained, they were so fussy about
warmth that he had to assign a member of his staff to take their
temperatures every day. How that was accomplished is, I feel, better left to the imagination. I suppose that poor soul stormed into
Hubble's office one day and fumed, "My mama didn't raise me to
be no . . . well, I can't rightly say what she would call this, but
you see my point."

So I gave up on the worms.

But I felt that, somehow, I had to show leadership in my yard.
So I embarked upon a new tradition of delivering, once a year, a
State of the Yard Address. I give it from the back porch, usually in
February, after the President gives his version. It is attended by
such family, friends, neighbors, Jehovah's Witnesses, and wild animals as are in the vicinity with time on their hands (or paws or
feelers).

It generally goes something like this:

Ladies, gentlemen, and assorted species,

Nowadays, scientists say the universe is crumbling, decaying,
falling part. They say that, many millions of years from now, the
universe will be a gooey, shapeless mess, with bits of Bridgeport
floating over near Andromeda and all whatnot, although things
will probably be so chaotic that terms such as "Bridgeport," "Andromeda," and even the old favorite "over near" may not be all
that useful or, for that matter, comprehensible.

At times like these, it is incumbent upon the individual homeowner to keep his own little patch of the universe in the most
coherent shape possible, even though in our yard the aforemen-
tioned process of disintegration seems to be moving a little faster
than it is elsewhere.

Out of chaos often comes hope. (Applause, growls.) It is possible to look at the yard and see bright new possibilities for a nascent suburban utopia. Or, failing that, at least for the kind of environment from which visiting service persons and guests do not have to be rescued with heavy emergency equipment.

Ha-ha. (Dead silence.)

All rhetoric and kidding aside, though, I'd like to take this moment to run through some key elements of our yard and update you on their status.

• The Sidewalk. The sidewalk, our link to the outside world, is of paramount importance. Only a fool or a mountebank would stand before you today and tell you the sidewalk is in great shape. One has to wonder about the wisdom of the Founders, who established the sidewalk in an area where water collects and freezes and melts and refreezes and heaves and erodes and deepens, until now it has become a great and mighty glacier, creeping forward inexorably, carving out cirques and tarns in the face of the earth and killing off the woolly mammoths and primitive ground sloths that once flourished here. Recent sonar studies indicate that the sidewalk is still under the ice somewhere, but the cost of reclaiming it may be prohibitive, and my administration intends to press forward with our proposal to let the water stand, order some exotic koi and a few ceramic frogs in the spring, and build a curved Japanese redwood bridge to the doorstep.

There is the additional bright prospect that the moles, who have been hard at work undermining the rest of the yard, may eventually drop it down to the level of the sidewalk, although the overall impact of that situation on our way of life is hard to imagine. That prospect, however, is neither here nor there, a description which pretty well sums up the sidewalk, now that I think of it.

• The Dog Pen. I said at the very outset of my term that it would be the goal of this administration to get the government off the dog's back. This strategy has worked, and today the dog is productively involved in any number of private-sector initiatives, ranging from the excavation of a large, indeed ominously man-sized, pit, to the gradual destruction of all vegetation in the pen, including several formerly mighty oaks. The dog has also painstakingly arranged in its pen a number of objects in a strangely druidic, Stonehengean pattern, but, when queried about this or anything else, the dog merely tilts its head and arches its eyebrows in an off-putting way.

• The Turf. Much has been made of this administration's autumnal failure to deliver on its promise to get all the leaves raked up before they welded themselves inseparably to the ground by dint of some insufficiently understood interbonding at the molecular level. The consequence of this lapse will remain a mystery until springtime, although periodic thaws have revealed alarming patches of quaking, brown protozoan life where once there was grass.

• Our Adversaries. Those of us who call this yard our home know that we are an ecosystem imperiled by the encroachment of others. While neighboring yard presidents have opted to lay down repellent chemicals of various sorts, we have not, which makes us look, to the huddled masses of domestic pests, like a veritable Ellis Island for bugs, mice, moles, and assorted others. (Grumbling.) Close on their heels are rogue cats, a little white dog who stands at our southern border and says "yurf" at three-second intervals all day long for some unknown reason, and some other creature with strange feet and pink, glowering eyes. Not to mention various forms of surly vegetation. A copy of G. Gordon Liddy's *Will* was wrested away from a cluster of seditious-looking plants not long ago.

• The Frontier. Our dreams turn ever to the West, where lies the great unclaimed area. The previous owner appears to have cut down a few trees, pawed the earth gingerly, and retreated to the safety of the porch. It is a harsh land, and only a rough people can tame it. At present, a small group of Tasaday tribespeople eke out a simple existence there. N!Gt'ala, their leader, seems like a decent-enough sort and has indicated, as near as I can tell, a willingness to discuss such points as cooperative use of the territory and even the recent disappearance of the man who came to fill our oil tank. (Applause, laughter, hissing.)

I Was a Teenage Vampire Flusher

As a newspaper columnist, I am sometimes chagrined because no killer has ever turned himself in to me. Surrendered himself, I mean. I don't suggest that a killer should try to become me. That would be devilish inconvenient.

I don't even insist on a killer. I would be willing to start with some kind of entry-level confession. A serial depositor of used chewing gum on the undersides of things would do.

NAB JACK THE MASTICATOR
Son Of
Spearmint
Yields to Pundit

So I confess to experiencing a morbid thrill when I found a message, scrawled by a secretary, on my desk one day. It said a man named Nick Kotula called. It also said "killed 28 hats in his house."

I tried to picture the haberdasherial carnage—a hamburger of homburgs. He snuck up behind the straw boater and filled it with grapeshot. And lured the derby into the clawfoot bathtub and then chucked a toaster in the drink. How did the Easter bonnet get it? In the conservatory with the candlestick, I'll hazard.

STOVEPIPE STALKER
SQUEALS TO SCRIBE
Local Fedoras Brim
With Gratitude

I called him back pronto, already turning book titles over in my head. *Tuque Kill a Mortarboard.* Hmmm, needs some work.

I reached Kotula's tape machine. It featured him singing Jerome Kern's "The Way You Look Tonight" and accompanying himself on the ukulele. He should keep his day job. In the background I could hear Kotula, live, yelling over the music that he was on the line.

When things settled down, Kotula said his friends had urged him to call me "about the twenty-eight bats I killed in my house."

Bats? I could have screamed.

MAN KILLS BATS

Blah.

28 BATS BRING
MESSAGE FROM ELVIS
TO TEN-GALLON KILLER

A little better.

Anyway, here's what happened. Nick was in bed watching Johnny Carson one night when a bat flew in the room.

"Hiyoooh!" said Johnny and Ed.

"Yargh!" said Nick. He ran like a bat out of Halifax, got his BB gun, and dispatched the critter.

On several subsequent nights, this adventure repeated itself. Nick got to be a pretty good shot, but his bedroom was being done over in BB holes and bat blood. He also knew not whence came the bats.

So Nick turned to the government. Feeling that he needed protection from the environment, he called the state Department of Environmental Protection.

Someone there offered to mail him the pamphlet "Bats in Connecticut." (There goes *that* title for a tragicomic novel.) Nick felt, given the probability that a bat would be stopping by that night to check out Doc Severinsen's outfit, this was a pretty weak gesture.

As the bat visitations continued, he developed a system. He'd snap at the bat with a towel to stun it, drop a coffee can over the prostrate chiropteran, slip the plastic lid on. Voilà. Bat in a Can. Chockful o' Bats.

Then Nick would shake the can until he was sure the bat was hors de combat. About thirty shakes, says Nick, although this is no magic number. Finally—kids, don't try this at home—Nick would flush the toilet "until I had a good whirlpool going" and send the bat to Davey Jones's Locker, or a noxious facsimile thereof.

It made Nick a little nervous about sitting on the toilet at first, but after a while, even that qualm drifted away. We humans are adaptable creatures. The whole process became just another humdrum household chore. Snap, can, shake, rattle, and flush. Back in bed before Charo's routine was over.

Still, in some part of Nick's soul, an inner voice was asking, Is this any way to live?

Also, how long before a bat with his number came along? In all probability, bats were training for him in some nearby guerrilla camp, snapping little towels at each other, dodging mock coffee cans, perfecting the Ninja Terminator Bat who would avenge his fallen comrades.

Nick called the state again and reached someone who told him to go up to his attic, where he would see a lot of bats hanging upside down. He could just peel them off the walls. None of this was true, but you get the feeling that that's what it says in Subsection 105.9(R7) of the Trilateral Bat Manual. Nick felt, overall, that the bureaucracy was not geared up to deal with the particulars of his crisis.

Life worsened. A bachelor, Nick could not invite guests over because "I had bats." Talk about a social disease.

Two months and twenty-eight dead bats later, Nick noticed his cat nosing at something in the fireplace. It was a baby bat. He looked up the flue and saw a pair of adult beady eyes.

Battle-seasoned for special weapons and tactics, Nick fetched his vacuum cleaner and endeavored to suck the monster down. No go.

(I always suspected those vacuum cleaner commercials where they show the bat being sucked down the chimney were probably fake.)

Nick boarded up his flue; the bats left; the chicks came back (but refused, after reading my story about Nick, to use his toilet, which kept their visits short).

And there our story ends. I'm not sure what the moral is.

ROTO-ROOTER VAMPIRE KILLER SAYS: JOHNNY MADE ME DO IT

The next time someone wants to turn himself in, I'm giving him Jimmy Breslin's number.

The Roar of the Fleecepaint
or
We Molted in New Haven: Tales of Animals in Show Business

In his classic treatise "Dogs in Opera: A Reassessment," the revered critic Frito Wolff-Funicello writes:

"The wisdom of the centuries urges us to search for dogs who epitomize the so-called big 'ences' of canine opera. These are patience, silence, and continence.

"Consider the lamentably heroic Schnauzer Menschenfeind, who departed from the script on the opening night of Marcel Igname's *Les Accountants Dégarnis d'Avignon* and rushed into the burning building to rescue the otherwise doomed lovers Claude and Croquette, thus spoiling Igname's tragic ending and persuading him to quit opera and take over his father-in-law's dry-cleaning establishment."

Actually, I made all that up.

There is not any scholarly writing on the subject of dogs in opera. There are not even any good parts for dogs in opera, although I was at work on an opera about Queen Elizabeth and her dogs, to be called *Corgi and Bess*, until someone told me that was not a new joke.

Nevertheless, as a veteran observer of animals in show business, I have even seen a corgi audition for an opera role. A local opera company had an open call for two dogs to appear in *La Bohème*. There is no pooch in Puccini, as written, but the opera figured, what the heck, you throw a dog in the show, you sell another twenty-five tickets right off the bat.

The dogs were to appear on alternating nights. All they had to do was walk onstage with the elegant Musetta and not bite anybody or join in the singing or exit prematurely.

This is not as easy as it might, on the surface, seem. An ordinarily reasonable dog may not be ready for opera unless its owners routinely walk around the house bellowing "Mascalzone!" at it and hitting high B's.

This was proven beyond all doubt at the audition as dog after dog lost composure (and, on one occasion, something considerably more visceral than composure) during the singing of the beautiful "Quando me'n vo" waltz.

Most of the dogs reacted to the high B in the aria as though a national dog emergency had just been declared. They wriggled free, looked around wildly, and, in some cases, bolted for the wings.

Other dogs committed such operatic faux pas as barking, whimpering, and swan-diving off the stage. One dog eliminated itself by eliminating, and another refused to do its stupid pet trick, while the owner stood there stomping, gesticulating, and yelling "Do it for Muhhhtherr."

It should be added that the sort of people who will bring their dogs to an opera audition tend not to own regular old dogs named Duke and Smoky. Mostly they own little fluffy dogs about the size a hamster on steroids. The dogs at the audition wore such monikers as Dark Crystal, Sassy, Little Joy San, and Chablis. Life ain't easy for a dog named Chablis.

"What kind of dog is that?" I asked one woman.

"Shih Tzu."

"Gesundheit," I wanted to say. Instead, I asked its name.

"Ho-Wing-Kwah."

"Wha'?"

"Ta-Pong-Woo."

"Who?"

My personal favorite was a huge collie named Magnum, mainly because of his cheerful gastronomic interest in the other contestants. He blew it by climbing up on the soprano, apparently in search of something more substantial than a good-night lick.

The redoubtable Po-Kwee-Tong was one of the two big winners, along with a cockapoo named Golda. I thought they were both a little highfalutin. It was my feeling that opera in general could be vastly improved by an infusion of populist dogs, but my feelings were not sounded out on this occasion or on many others.

If you think, however, that my experience with auditioning animals begins and ends on so pedestrian a note as dogs in opera, you misjudge me. I have, for instance, watched peacocks audition for modern dance.

The Sankai Juku dance troupe of Japan used to do a number—and maybe they still do—which called for a peacock. They didn't travel with their own bird—probably tough to get them through the metal detector—so every night it was another town, another peacock.

When the troupe played New Haven a couple of years back, the Shubert had an open call for peacocks. As a journalist and of an inquiring mind, I was invited to attend. Four peacocks showed up. (The notice specified dancing peacocks only, which probably kept a lot of singing peacocks away.) They all belonged to a well-off West Havenite who had sent them over, along with his caretaker and de facto peafowl wrangler, one Bert LeBeau or Lebeau (see below), a grizzled man wearing a baseball cap bedecked with many, many buttons, some of them reflecting certain aspects of Bert's world view. One of the buttons said, "Be Healthy, Eat Your Honey."

Sitting here now, I find myself wishing John Ruskin's observation that "the most beautiful things in the world are useless; peacocks and lilies for instance" could be squeezed onto a button and slipped onto Bert's starry diadem. But as my grandmother used to say, "If wishes were peacocks, who would clean up after them?"

As I sat in the darkness of the lushly appointed Shubert, the casting director called out, "We're ready for Peacock Number One."

Clatter, clatter, clatter. The peacock's hard little talons on a flat

floor sounded like Mr. Bojangles doing a tap step. The bird appeared onstage wearing a little "1" sign around its neck, which
made it look like someone at a very peculiar dance marathon.

By chance or theatrical instinct, Peacock Number One wan-
dered out to stage center and clattered down to the proscenium,
right about where you'd want to be for your big solo—which, in
the case of Number One, seemed to consist of shifting from foot to
foot and swiveling its head back and forth quite anxiously.

"I really need this job, I gotta have this job . . ." I sang, in-
wardly.

I asked Bert if the peacocks have names.

"No," he said.

Why not? I asked.

"I don't name 'em," he said, firmly.

It occurred to me that daily contact with peacocks may wear a
man down in certain ways. For instance, Bert claimed to have no
opinion about whether or not the *b* in his own last name should be
capitalized.

"Doesn't matter," he insisted. "Still the same name."

You might go a long time, if you did not travel in peacock-
infested circles, before you found another person who did not care
how his name was spelled.

In time, Peacock Number Two was summoned. Its concept of
the role turned out to be somewhat different. Number Two scut-
tled onstage, looked around at the whole setup, and took off like a
bat out of Worcester, coming to a messy landing in Row M, Seat
29.

Don't call us, we'll call you.

Number Three was summoned. It repeated Number Two's performance, with the new wrinkle of flying straight at Row G, Seat
22, where I happened to be sitting until my lightning-quick re-
flexes took over and sent me sprawling to the floor. We chroniclers
of exotic-bird modern dance auditions live in the teeth of danger.
Don't let nobody tell you different.

You would think, wouldn't you, that Number Four would have
settled on a new tack, but it was intent on joining its fellows.
Abruptly, the Shubert had an Audubon Society nightmare on its

hands, with three peacocks flapping around in the aisles, bashing into things, molting enough feathers to stuff a futon, and generally maculating the formerly immaculate theater appointments.

Looks 10, Continence 3.

The dauntless LeBeau eventually rounded them up and got them settled down, all except Number Four, who immediately walked straight off the stage and fell kerplunk into the orchestra pit.

Bert fished Number Four out. Intent on proving Ruskin right, Number Four retraced its steps and fell kerplunk again, raising questions about its chances for a Life in the Theater, not to mention its learning ability.

In the midst of all this, we suddenly noticed that Number One had never stopped placidly hoofing around under the spotlight.

"Look at that, a real show-biz bird," one of the Shubert guys said.

A star is born.

I never saw the peacock or the opera dogs perform, but I hear everything went great. Still, it is one thing to train dogs, peacocks, elephants, tigers, piranhas, etc., to behave in an orderly, yea, even obliging, fashion. But when you start talking about training pigeons, well, that's a whole other ball of wax. Pigeons are probably just about the least obliging animals in the cosmos, except for spitting cobras. (Come to think of it, Marlin Perkins did not hesitate to mess around with spitting cobras, but you never saw him take on a pigeon.)

Why, at the newspaper which employs me, we come up against pigeons who make the Kurdish rebels look like pussycats. They have claimed the eaves of the local interstate highway—which, unhappily, overhangs our parking lot—as their fortress, and there is no driving them out.

I recall that our Human Resources Department, back when it was the Personnel Department, attempted to scare them away by putting fake owls up there. The fake owls were never heard from again. I believe the pigeons mailed a severed fake owl ear back to us, along with a snarky note.

So the concept of trained pigeons is almost more than I can grasp.

I am probably the closest thing to a pigeon trainer around here, having, as a small boy, picked up a pigeon in my hands and brought it into my grandmother's apartment. I am not sure what I had in mind, but I was not given the opportunity to train the pigeon to do anything except leave, which it did, after staging a scene which was, now that I think of it, an eerie foreshadowing of the Shubert peacock imbroglio.

With all of the above in mind, I seized the opportunity, when it was offered a while back, to meet Antoaneta Romanovi, who enthralls the multitudes at the Ringling Brothers and Barnum & Bailey Circus with her trained pigeons.

Many-colored tinted pigeons.

And little poodles.

The pigeons hop on a big shiny ball, ride bicycles and other little contraptions, and perch on the arms of a standing-up poodle.

It's nice. It's kind of a relief after the elephants and whatnot.

Antoaneta is—I make bold to say—a great-looking woman and very nice. She is Bulgarian.

Most people in the circus are from foreign countries, possibly because there aren't such strict laws overseas against placing a very light person at one end of a seesaw and having four much heavier people jump on the other end.

That trend, however, makes me worry that we, as a nation, are slipping in certain life-enhancing fields. We're getting so that all we know is semiconductor chips, fast food, and overhead cam engines, but we have no facility with pigeons or sword-swallowing.

One way to start catching up would be to initiate a national campaign in which all Americans, when they finish a task (be it welding a trailer hitch or restructuring an annuity), would yell "Hey!"

I suppose I could suggest this to the Reagan administration, but then they have their own ideas about how to run a circus.

Anyway, back to Antoaneta, who got into pigeons and poodles because her husband thought it would be a nice act for a woman, especially compared to the main Romanovi family act, which involves performing various rupture-inviting feats aboard horses racing at breakneck speeds.

Antoaneta told me this through her daughter Madlen, who is also—I make bold again—nice-looking and is no stranger to pigeons. Madlen was on hand as a translator, although both women seemed to speak the same brand of pleasantly off-kilter English. They only succeeded in making me lose track of who said what.

The pigeons, they explained, are dipped in food coloring. As long as you stop at the neck, "It's okay, they don't mind."

Speaking of mind, pigeons, according to the Romanovis, "Don't have brains too much."

Following in the doughty footsteps of Bert, the Romanovis do not give their pigeons names. This was an easy decision to make because pigeons do not have personality too much either.

I asked them if any of the pigeons especially crave the limelight and clamor for more stage time.

"Pigeons, no," I was told. "They don't understand from this nothing."

This is not to say that pigeons don't have any concept of, say, morality. They mate for life, according to the Bulgarian gals, and are very choosy when picking out a mate.

On the other hand, traveling with them is no day at the beach, unless you happen to be at the beach for a day. "When it is hot, they have so much fights," Antoaneta informed me matter-of-factly, "because they start make love."

Ah.

Madlen seemed to feel that, in my ceaseless probings into the pigeon psyche, I was overlooking the crucial difficulty one faces in assembling a poodle and pigeon act, which, she said quite seriously, is, "It's so hard to teach the dogs not to eat the pigeons."

I imagine the learning process is quite hard on the pigeons.

The pigeons, I found out, are also of Bulgarian origin. What if one defected? Would the Audubon people get involved?

Those are interesting questions, but perhaps not as interesting as another set of questions dogging the circus in those days. Those questions were:

1. Is it fair to lead a person to believe he is seeing a unicorn when in fact all he is seeing is a goat who has been induced to make certain personal sacrifices?

2. Is this any way to treat a goat?

I speak, naturally, of the notorious and so-called unicorn displayed by the Ringling Brothers and Barnum & Bailey Circus (which has somehow come to seem more like the name of a Wall Street brokerage firm than a gaudy extravaganza).

I was kind of disappointed that the unicorn was not traveling with the particular circus company in which Antoaneta's pigeons performed. I am attracted to philosophical questions like the two above, and one look into the unicorn's eyes would have helped me a great deal to formulate my own personal answers.

Strictly speaking, a unicorn is a mythological horselike beast with a single horn protruding from its noggin. A lion's tail is optional. Taxes, licensing, and dealer prep not included.

Persons of science adjudged the circus unicorn to be a goat who was surgically altered so that one of its natural horns would grow out of the middle of its head.

My hat is off to the RB&B&BC if they can get a goat to add any sort of luster to an occasion. I have nothing against goats, but I never met one who, in my judgment, seemed capable of bringing off a unicorn impersonation. Or even a halfway decent Jimmy Stewart.

Unicorns are supposed to be romantic and graceful and mysterious.

A goat is none of those things. Magic from a goat is blood from a stone. Every goat I have ever met—and I am no stranger to goats—has acted as though just getting through the day was a fifty-fifty proposition at best. A goat is so thoroughly grounded in its goatness that it is incapable of pretending to be something more.

The goat/unicorn also represented some fairly muddled iconographic thinking by the circus. Unicorns traditionally have been a symbol of virginity. (Mostly, this is because there is so little networking among unicorns. Statistics, in fact, indicate that a virgin unicorn over thirty has a better chance of being burned by a dragon than of, as they say in Bulgaria, making love.)

Goats, on the other hand, have tended to lean in the opposite direction, symbolism-wise.

In fact, John Donne wondered, not unreasonably,

If lecherous goats, if serpents envious
Cannot be damned; alas; why should I be?

It was kind of gratifying, in a meanspirited way, to discover the black heart of vivisection lying under the glossy surfaces of the RB&B&BC. In recent years, that circus has become pretty buttoned-down, white-bread stuff—in sharp Lysol-disinfected contrast to the darkling, scummy circuses of my youth.

I guess we should all rejoice that the RB&B&BC's tastes in mythological animals do not run to griffins and manticores. I bet they'd be stapling and gluing eagles and lions and scorpions and gorillas together in all sorts of horrible ways.

The American Society for the Prevention of Cruelty to Animals did not see fit to rejoice. No indeed. The ASPCA urged animal lovers to boycott the circus until this wrong is righted.

Somehow.

That's just it. What can the RB&B&BC do to make it right? Saw off the horn? Drop the goaticorn from the show? The only thing worse than a vivisected unigoat is an unemployed one. Four, actually. The circus apparently carried three backup unicorns (all dreaming, no doubt, of that classic show-biz break when the star comes down with hoof-and-mouth disease and the understudy steps in and . . .).

No, no, it won't do. We can't have mythological animals walking our city streets, unemployed, bitter, brooding over the glory that was once theirs. (The roar of the fleecepaint . . .) And you can't send them back to the farm once they've seen Paree, so to speak.

I'd like to know what the circus paid the goats. Unicorn scale? I'd like to think the goats had a little nest egg (if unicorns have eggs) put aside for the day the circus tires of them and casts them aside. Alex the dog, I read somewhere, got $317.40 a day for a not-very-good beer commercial. A unigoat ought to be worth at least that.

Who is to say where the circus will stop, given all the attention they got from this one project? By the time their shameless lust for oddities is quenched, we may have lived to see a pig with antlers, a monkey with wings, an actuary with personality.

It doesn't bear thinking about.

The Up Side of a Downhill Bear

A guy was telling me one day what I should do about my moles. In the ground, I mean. Not a dermatological conversation. I am always asking people what I should do about my moles. I expect that, if you got me in to see the Pope, I would swing the discussion around to moles pretty darned quick.

But this is not a chapter on moles. I am kind of holding off on them, waiting to see if the moles and I achieve any kind of denouement. If there is not any separate chapter on moles in this book, you will know that we reached our private Armageddon and the moles won. Carry on the fight without me.

Anyway, this guy was telling me this about moles and that about moles, and we really weren't getting anywhere. And he happened to say, "Funny we should be talking about moles. I hear there's a bear loose in Tariffville today."

For a moment I thought "bear" was some kind of inside term among avid mole observers for a certain especially large kind of mole. Then I realized he meant, by "bear," what I understood "bear" to mean. (Okay, okay, if you wanted semiotics, you would have bought Umberto Eco's book.)

We don't get many bears in Connecticut, so I decided I better drive up and try to see this one. I thought about stopping to pick up my bear-sniffing (well, he might be) dog Roy, since it was an educational opportunity for him.

Also, Roy looks, from certain angles, like a bear (as well as like several other animals)—which might come in handy if the bear became annoyed at the lack of bear-oriented activities in Tariffville.

Time, however, is of the essence in bear coverage. So I went alone.

Tariffville is a great place for a bear. A village tucked up by the hairpin of the Farmington River, it does not seem to belong to the towns around it or, for that matter, to any recent decade. It's a rough-and-ready little place, and it feels like the end of the line. If a bear put on a T-shirt and a Shakespeare fishing tackle baseball cap, he could get along fine in Tariffville without drawing much notice.

My fear was that the bear would work south to some of the nearby tony suburbs, where the economy is based principally on pâté and where a bear might mistake a bottle of honey-fenugreek chelating shampoo for an aperitif, with dire consequences. Bears are pretty amiable, but there is no telling what a bear, gorged unto constipation on upscale blueberry cheesecake, might do.

After wandering around town looking for the bear and not seeing much, I stopped in at a local drinking establishment. The years have taught me that I am not the type of shirt-sleeves reporter who can walk into a bar and get folks to jaw with me real naturallike.

But I sat down in the midst of the regulars and inquired heartily, "So! Anyone see this bear?"

There was a general edging away from me.

A waitress came over. "Get many bears in here?" I asked.

"Nope. We do get a few animals," she retorted slyly.

Things were picking up.

I talked to one guy who didn't believe me. About anything. He pointed out that he had a six-year degree and that I wasn't talking to a fool. He asked to see some identification. I showed him some. He said, "Huh." He said he'd been all over the gorges and he could show me some places. But he didn't believe there was any bear. He reminded me that he had a six-year degree. I said I knew that. He said, "Richard, isn't it?" Colin, I said. He said he could show me some places.

I left and continued to move around Tariffville, keenly aware that I was several steps behind the bear and people who had actually seen it. But I had no trouble locating folks who knew somebody who had seen the bear.

I found Carole Newton, wearing a Commie Busters T-shirt, up at the Tree House Nursery, where there is a sign saying GUARD DOG ON DUTY TWO NIGHT [sic] A WEEK. GUESS WHICH NIGHT. Someone told Carole about the bear, and she told a couple of mechanics, who laughed at her, climbed in their truck, drove down the road, and did one of those look-at-the-size-of-that-dog-hey-wait-a-minute takes.

I walked down to a field where some people said the bear had been. Standing out there on the naked Connecticut veldt, I found myself getting very nervous, in an *Out of Tariffville* kind of way, about the great distance to my car and the absence of M'challah, my faithful gun-bearer.

I went back to the bar, where—if they had a lick of sense—they would have jumped on the promotional opportunity by serving Grizzly beer and advertising "the paws that refreshes," etc.

By now, word had spread, and the bear was the news of the day. There were, as there will be, some newly minted bear experts in the bar, and I got into a rousing discussion with some guy about the fact that bears can run uphill better than downhill (or vice versa) because their front legs are longer than their hind legs (or something like that). We ordered more beer and tried to pin down our feelings on this subject. Eventually, we achieved general agreement that (a) bears can run in one direction faster than the other and (b) it has something to do with leg length, front vis-à-vis back.

"Wait a minute," the guy, suddenly sure about this, interjected. "It's downhill. They can't run downhill fast. These guys told me if you're ever chased by a bear, run downhill." (Author's note: I'm guessing the guys, whoever they might be, would advise you just to avoid bears entirely in flat regions.)

"That's useful to know," I said beerily. "Lemme write that down."

"Well," he said, only a trifle abashedly, "check your references on that."

Bear or no bear, you got to love Tariffville.

Rumor had it the bear was over near Old St. Andrew's Episcopal Church, a beautiful little white structure in the heart of (nowadays) bear country. I hustled over there, hoping at least for a theological perspective on bears, but the rector was out, so I went home.

The bear eluded pursuit for days and hastened across Connecticut. People who saw him said he looked quite purposeful, like the White Rabbit. He was apprehended near a Baptist church in Rhode Island. They shot him with a tranquilizer gun and drove him up to New Hampshire. I guess we should be grateful. Given the theological drift he seemed to be taking, he could have wound up as Pat Robertson's running mate.

Possibly the bear was after a little theological perspective on humans. In Isaiah 59:11, it is written, "We roar all like bears, and mourn sore like doves: we look for judgment, but there is none; for salvation, but it is far off from us."

I believe Isaiah is silent on the uphill/downhill debate, but I haven't, as they say in Tariffville, checked my references on that.

The President's Dog Is Fired

U.S. presidents have usually felt a need to own dogs, with mixed results.

Dogs are honest, and I suppose that's why presidents like them. A U.S. President is much too powerful to be told the truth by anyone else. But so much of a presidential administration is based on guile that a guileless dog may be eternally out of sync with its surroundings.

Our memories of presidential dogs are tainted. LBJ hoisting his dog by the ears (and himself by a corresponding petard). Nixon and Checkers, who (many of us have subconsciously come to believe) was rented for the occasion.

I believe Ford and Carter had dogs, but it is hard to remember whose was whose. It's the same way with the kids. Except for Amy, nobody can really rattle off the names of the Ford and Carter offspring. ("Lemme see. There was Chip . . . Robbie . . . Ernie. No, those were 'My Three Sons.' . . . One of them definitely had a son named Chip, right? And an Ernie? Ernie Ford? No, that's Tennessee Ernie Ford I'm thinking of. . . . Chip, Robin, Barry, Maurice . . . Was one of Carter's kids married to Lulu?") And so on. To make matters worse, every time I think I remember something Carter's dog might have done, I'm never completely sure it wasn't Billy.

Still, I believe the Reagan administration has a sorrier record with dogs than just about any previous White House tenant. Ronald Reagan is certainly the first President ever to fire his dog. I refer, of course, to the misnamed Lucky, who was banished from the White House to the Santa Barbara ranch when he became too much to handle. Reagan subsequently offered some kind of weasely explanation for the whole affair, which made me think even less of him. Truman at least had the guts to fire MacArthur straight out.

Dogs tend to remind us of our limitations as mortals. I believe that was Lucky's big offense.

On the other hand, the Reagan administration hasn't been any too thorough about reminding dogs of their limitations as dogs. Consider the publication, several years back, of *C. Fred's Story—A Dog's Life* by C. Fred Bush, "edited slightly by Barbara Bush."

That would be Barbara Bush, wife of Vice-President George Bush. And that would be C. Fred Bush, cocker spaniel of Vice-President George Bush.

I don't think it's particularly appropriate to dwell on exactly who published this book. Why tarnish an otherwise fine company which has gone on to undertake other, more meritorious projects involving promising young authors whose very financial stability depends on acceptance of their current manuscripts? (Okay, okay, it was Doubleday.)

The news that George Bush's dog had published a book would doubtless have been greeted by nosegays and huzzahs had it not suffered from unfortunate timing. It had just then become known that William Kennedy's *Ironweed* had been turned down by thirteen publishers before finding its way into print and winning the Pulitzer Prize. It didn't seem likely that ol' C. Fred had paid the same kind of dues, padding up and down the Avenue of the Americas with an increasingly saliva-drenched manuscript in his jaws. But life—to use a coinage later made popular by C. Fred's co-author—is something that rhymes with rich.

Yes, I did read it, and I can save you some time. The book is dumb. The dog is spoiled. The prospect of C. Fred and his doting mistress sitting one heartbeat away from First Familyhood does nothing for one's mental composure.

To be fair about it, the proceeds were to be donated to two

literacy organizations, and Barbara Bush put a statement on the jacket urging us all to take the problem of illiteracy seriously.

To be mean about it, only the Reagan administration would ask us to take illiteracy seriously in the context of a book written by a cocker spaniel. And a rich, pampered cocker spaniel at that. Not a cocker spaniel who knows the hungry, jangled poetry of life in the streets.

The only solace to be found in this trend—if that's what it is—is the possibility, however slim, that the hapless Lucky might somehow be able to write his side of the story, but I believe measures are being taken to keep Kitty Kelley away from him.

However, when Ronald Reagan sits down to write his memoirs, you can bet an entire volume will be devoted to the Lucky crisis, a volume perhaps titled *A Time to Heel.* Herewith are some excerpts I have more or less fabricated in the privacy of my brain:

DAY 1. Members of the White House staff met with me in the Oval Office at 9:23 A.M. and alerted me to the fact that my slippers had been chewed up. Still groggy at the early hour, I rubbed the sleep from my eyes and asked Don Regan to prepare a damage report on the slippers. Could they be repaired? If not, what interim arrangements could we make until replacements could be found?

Regan had anticipated me. He told me GSA paracobblers were already on the scene and that preliminary estimates listed the left slipper as "totaled" and the right slipper as "viable on a make-do basis."

Armed with this information, we began to formulate options.

Larry Speakes voiced alarm at the scenario of me walking around in one slipper, which, he said, could impact on my credibility, plus I might catch cold. I was inclined to agree. I asked Michael Deaver to serve as point man on the slipper situation, reminding him that it would have to be resolved one way or the other by 10 P.M., when I would be changing out of my shoes.

Setting my jaw, I looked around the room at the tough and resourceful men I had assembled as a team to see me through just this very sort of dilemma. "What I am trying to say, gentlemen, is that while this Lucky thing continues to embroil us, there is little possibility that I will be taking an afternoon nap."

DAY 2: On our morning walk, Lucky abruptly broke stride and dragged me into the Rose Garden, where I suffered numerous thorn-related abrasions. Upon our return to the White House, he raced into the office, leaped on my desk, and left muddy paw prints all over some critical "white papers" requiring my attention. I called him a bad dog. He barked excitedly at me and raced down to the James Polk half-bath, where he seized the end of the toilet paper in his mouth and raced down the hall, unrolling toilet paper as he went.

I summoned Robert "Bud" McFarlane to my office. We agreed that Lucky had committed acts of aggression. I told "Bud" I wanted to send a message to dogs everywhere that I would not countenance this sort of thing on American soil. Don Regan came in at this time and asked if the Lucky crisis had in fact become a situation and, if so, whether we should start meeting in the Situation Room. I asked Charles Wick to play devil's advocate and argue that it wasn't a situation, but after five minutes of picking apart the idea that it was a situation ("It's not a situation; it's really not," I remember him saying), Charlie caved in and allowed as how he, all along, had felt it was.

Don Regan then revealed that the Situation Room was full of boxes of stuff he hadn't gotten around to unpacking and that it might take a while for aides to move them all out into the hall. My heart sank at this blow, because I knew it would sap the enthusiasm and emotional momentum which had been building among my staff over the prospect of going to the Situation Room. Looking around the room at the gaunt, haggard faces of men who, in many cases, had slept only six hours the previous night and were now working straight through the afternoon, I saw my worst fears confirmed.

Turning to Don, I set my jaw and said, "We've got a disobedient dog on our hands here. I want those boxes out in twenty minutes How you accomplish that is your problem."

Immediately, the mood lifted. We agreed to pursue a policy of "constructive fatigue" in which we tried to tire Lucky out. Feeling it was no longer appropriate to keep the legislative branch in the dark, I phoned Bob Dole at the Senate and asked him to come over and throw a Frisbee for Lucky so I could have a couple of hours to myself.

Failing to comprehend the seriousness of the crisis, Bob allowed as how he was pretty busy with tax reform, but I countered that others were being asked to make sacrifices in the national interest and that Justice Rehnquist had thrown a tennis ball for two hours the day before.

DAY 3: A whole chicken disappeared from a cutting board in the White House kitchen. I summoned Cap Weinberger to the Situation Room and told him there was mounting concern over who was going to take Lucky out. Cap said he could have tactical units of Marine commandos and Navy SEALS choppered in within minutes to take Lucky out. "Those fellas will lay down so much mortar fire that you won't even find a bark left when the smoke clears," he enthused.

I explained that I had only meant "take him out for a walk." Cap seemed crestfallen, so I reassured him that I did not rule out forcible actions if the crisis escalated. He brightened a little at this flicker of hope.

Dashed off a note to Deaver: "New slippers not comfortable. Stay on top of problem. Be prepared to exercise suede option."

DAY 4: Asked George Bush, whose dog has written a book, to backstop me on the Lucky initiative. We brainstormed on it for several hours, and George suggested giving Lucky an ambassadorship to Chad or Oman and making it look like a promotion. I said I didn't know either one of those guys, but I didn't guess they would put up with Lucky for long.

George Shultz demurred, arguing that we should demonstrate that we can solve the problem at home and that, anyway, he was tired of having all of this administration's scratch-and-dent items dumped on his ambassadorial corps. "Speak softly and carry a big rolled-up newspaper," he concluded.

I dozed off at one point and awoke to find everyone gone and my trouser cuffs inexplicably damp.

DAY 5: A White House maid greeted me with the news that there was a mistake on my desk. I chuckled and told her it wasn't the first time that had happened, and she arched her eyebrows. When I reached the office, however, I discovered her meaning and immediately went looking for Lucky. I found him in the William Henry Harrison den, where he had chewed up great quantities of the Millard Fillmore paneling.

I went upstairs and asked Nancy if she still had the tiny little gun I gave her.

Hoofing for Mr. Goodbard

Perhaps the most arresting news photograph from 1986 was the one from Shrewsbury, Vermont, where a wild moose had gone all moony over a moo cow.

Perhaps "wild" is too strong a word. The moose appeared on a Saturday in the cow pasture of one Larry Carrara and commenced to stare at one of Larry's cows, the fair Jessica. All day Saturday did the moose stare. And Sunday, Monday, Tuesday . . . It can take quite a while for a moose to think up an icebreaker.

"They've nuzzled like they're kissing, but I ain't seen no action," was Carrara's quote in a Wednesday-morning Associated Press item.

By Wednesday night, however, Carrara could be heard on National Public Radio saying that there had been "gestures."

"What kind of gestures?" the radio person asked.

"Gestures. This is a family show, ain't it?" Carrara retorted.

"Is she a pretty cow?" the radio person wanted to know.

"Got red hair. Blue eyes," said Carrara.

Carrara's rhetorical flair, I believe, has been wasted, tucked away on that Vermont farm.

In the photograph, moose and cow looked, to an alarming degree, like a married human couple in late middle age, photographed while vacationing with other members of a fraternal organization.

It was, in fact, mating season for moose. One theory was that lady mooses are in short supply up Shrewsbury way. Like so many of his fellow creatures, the moose had been obliged to adjust his expectations.

Several things have not, until now, been widely known: The moose's name is Jim. His heart, it turns out, is full of poetry for Jessica. And hers for him. The poetry Jessica and Jim wrote during their days together in the Vermont pasture has just been released to the public by the Department of Agriculture.

In my capacity as Assistant National Poet Laureate for Moose Affairs, I have been asked to share and discuss some of the love poems authored by these two remarkable animals.

We begin with "Lines Composed Just Outside Shrewsbury by Jim the Moose at 6 A.M. EST Upon Seeing the Loveliest Animal, Excluding Actual Moose Ladies, in the Universe," which was written in the so-called early period (Saturday to mid-Sunday), when Jim was still groping for meter and imagery to express his feelings.

O!
Hoof and horn,
My rapture is—
Ooommaauugghooooooh!

It was, admittedly, a poor beginning, one which would attract the scorn of such local critics as Trumaine Boblotboro, who, speaking at the Shrewsbury Koffee Korner, commented, "It don't have the kind of structure and sophistication of other—Billy, you wanna pass the maple syrup?—moose poems, for all its Whitmanesque gusto. Personally, I got to hope something more neoclassical is in the offing— Billy, I coulda tapped my own tree by now."

Boblotboro's words proved prophetic. By Monday, Jim had written "Wherefore Hereford," widely considered a masterpiece of quadruped romantic verse.

Flies, flies, my love, I am head-bitten.
Nostril-flared, I stand here smitten.
Moose heart engorged with sudden blood
For her who lingers over cud.

I hear my inner clock now tick.
I wait in hope for one cowlick.
From Olympic heights, in animal guise,
Did often come the philandering Zeus,
So why am I, [word untranslatable from moose language]
    eyes,
Just another randy moose?

Thus, in such short order, did Jim establish himself as a moose
poet of the—no, let us drop that qualifier—as a poet of the first
rank. Even as that happened, Jessica was readying herself to burst
forth with her own offering, which would cause at least one per-
ceptive critic to describe her and Jim as "the Brownings on the
hoof."

Here, in full, is Jessica's poem "Udderings," redolent of finger-
popping cadences from the Beat era.

Dig—
Here comes a dude in a driftwood derby
With all the pizzazz of a Durwood Kirby
Says I've got eyes with a special twinkle
Sounds like a load of his best bullwinkle
My mama's out to pasture, my daddy's in a daze
Wait 'til I tell 'em, "Guess who's coming to graze."

In the end, the impossibility of a life with Jessica drove itself
into Jim's consciousness and, some would say, crushed some of the
soaring lyricism there. He retreated to the Vermont woods where,
judging from the sparse output which has reached anthologists, his
poetry has become increasing snarled in a spiral of intellectualized
futility.

A sample:

I guess I don't know what I'm talking about.
I guess I don't even know what I mean
When I say I don't know what I'm talking about.

Jessica has contented herself with producing milk and the occasional wistful rondel.

The Kohlrabi Inheritance

The Food and Drug Administration has approved the sale of fruits and vegetables treated with low levels of radiation to inhibit spoilage. The following represents but one of the many horrifying, if untrue, consequences of that policy.

•

One problem we have now is, the radishes aren't afraid of the dog.

They were in the bedroom this morning when I woke up.

"Get out," I screamed and heard them all scuttle toward the closet.

I threw a dirty look over at the dog. "Can't stand up to a few lousy radishes, huh?"

The dog hung his head. Actually, he hasn't been the same since the spinach attacked him in the hallway.

We are all a little worn out these days. Last night, I microwaved an eggplant and brought it to the table. The top opened up and a smaller eggplant got out and then the top of that one opened up and an even smaller one got out and so on, until a little tiny man with hair as white as snow got out of the last eggplant and marched back and forth on our table playing "The Blue Bells of Scotland" on teeny-weeny bagpipes.

"I don't mind this once in a while but . . . ." My wife sighed.

Anyway, I grabbed a shower, squeezing in next to the broccoli in the tub.

"How you doin'?" I asked it.

"Aw, gee, I'm feeling a little, I don't know, deciduous these days," the broccoli said. It was reading a pamphlet titled *Hollandaise Sauce—Threat or Menace?*

"You oughta get out more," I advised. Truth is, the broccoli is the only vegetable around here I have any use for. It's polite and not too proud to pitch in with the chores.

The dad-blasted radishes were on my towel when I got out. "Get off!"

"Downstairs is kind of a mess," the broccoli said. "A few of those Georgia onions you brought home drank all the gas out of the weed whacker, and things got out of hand."

I shuffled through the poker chips and onion skin on the living-room carpet and went out to check the Great Blue Wheezing Cauliflower.

We had been keeping the GBWC chained down, like Prometheus, in the backyard, until the government inspectors showed up to deal with it. In the last three days, it had swelled to fourteen feet in diameter and had begun to emit heat.

So I was pretty shocked to look out the window and see a great steaming hole in the ground where the GBWC had been.

The front doorbell rang and I ran to get it, followed by the excited rustle of radish tendrils. I looked out the peephole and saw Brice Whipsaw, the government agent.

"Brice," I cried, opening the door.

"Whipsaw, U.S. Produce Episode Control Tactics. I understand we have an episode here."

"An episode?"

"A situation. A transient."

"You mean the cauliflower?"

"We're on top of it," Whipsaw said. "I'm running in cable, setting up geodesic domes, patching in to satellites. I've ordered microtomes, filament, aneroid barometers, deerstalker caps, silica gel, calipers, charts with tricolor acetate overlays, pointers, Orvis tackle bags, Swiss army knives, beef jerky, hydrogenated linseed oil. . . . We're here for the duration. This is nothing. Ask me about the celery in Twin Forks. Ask me about the snow peas in Pass Christian."

"What about them?"

"Don't ask."

Along about then my plumber, Pete, who calls me Tom, climbed out of the cauliflower hole.

"I don't know, Tom, I just don't know," he said, shaking his head. "That thing is pretty well tied in to your system now. I got it loose from the downstairs toilet, but don't use the sink until I come back with a bazooka and some cheese sauce."

"I can bring in state-of-the-art lead-lined gratin pans," Whipsaw cut in. "Ask me how they worked in Rochester."

"I see you got radishes, Tom," Pete added. "Try some borax on 'em."

The radishes chirped worriedly and hid behind my legs. Actually, I am getting kind of attached to the radishes.

"I've got the National Guard monitoring carp in nearby streams," said Whipsaw. "If they get bigger than forty inches, we evacuate and declare this ground zero. We can't let a blue cauliflower episode drag on. Ask me about Passaic."

We decided not to.

Wings and Prayers

Large birds in the house are not a good idea.

A woman of my acquaintance attended a house party several decades ago and, upon opening the refrigerator there, found an owl blinking unhappily at her.

She inquired about this and was told that someone had fed the owl too many martinis. It had been placed in the fridge for a brief spell to settle it down.

This is an extreme case, but it raises questions about the ability of people and large birds to live in harmony.

The local shopping circulars around here usually contain, every week, at least one or two advertisements from people seeking to unload their parrots.

There is something quietly desperate about the ads, and one often has cause to wonder if the whole truth is being told.

"FREE to good home. 2½-year-old parrot. Very special bird needs a very special person. Familiarity with Schopenhauer a must. Comes with cage, food dish, swagger stick, 41.8 lw Flusskrebs-Macheimer tropical bird tranquilizer gun. Please call. OK, we'll throw in $100 and an Ottoman. Like new."

An ad such as that provokes questions, not the least of which is whether the Ottoman is a footstool or a Turk.

There is probably no worse match, however, than a parrot and

psychotherapists. My friends, Vince and Annie, who are psychotherapists, own a parrot named Popsicle Pete.

Vince is a burly, passionate Italian guy from Queens. Annie is
an equally vivacious Jewish woman from Brooklyn.

Popsicle Pete is a crusty parrot. I don't know where he's from.

The parrot detests Annie, and has mixed feelings about Vince,
possibly because Vince will sometimes grab the parrot's terrifying
wire-cutter beak and cry, "I'm a green chicken! I'm a green
chicken!"

Vince is a psychiatrist and ought to know better. Who can even
guess at the resentment building up inside a parrot addressed as a
green chicken?

Vince and the parrot have had a very tempestuous relationship.
There was a time when they were in the habit of touching their
tongues together in a kiss. Popsicle Pete, however, seized an occasion of intimacy to bite Vince in the face, possibly out of residual
anger over this whole green chicken business. Vince responded,
reflexively, by slapping Popsicle Pete. Things have never been the
same.

Popsicle Pete's only unalloyed affection, then, is reserved for
Vince's aged father, who lives on the premises. Vince's father, in
turn, has reached a point in his life where a parrot is about as much
company as he wants, a good deal of the time.

In the mornings, Popsicle Pete generally climbs off his perch
and walks a stately waddle down the hall to the old man's bedroom
to greet his boon companion and begin a day of mutual crustiness.

Vince keeps Popsicle Pete's wings clipped, so that he can take
him outside without fear of losing him. (This is not a fear shared
by Annie, who would not regret the concomitant loss of a few
sticks of furniture should the earth ever open up and swallow the
parrot.)

One summer morning, Pete demonstrated to everyone that he
possessed a few more feathers than anyone had suspected. He flew
off Vince's shoulder for parts unknown. Green chicken this, bub.

Many people saw Vince and Annie that morning driving
around town in their golf cart—I forget why they have one—still
wearing pajamas, holding up a birdcage, beseeching the heavens

and sobbing. Vince was sobbing because he loves Popsicle Pete, despite their difficulties, and because he feared the parrot might never come back. Annie was sobbing because she hates to feel left out and because she feared it might.

No one has ever proved it, but I wonder if she had maybe even been showing Popsicle Pete brochures for alternative bird careers. (See the world! Eat garbage! Be a sea gull.)

About twenty-four hours and many, many tribulations—including the fruitless rental of a cherry picker for several hundred dollars—later, Popsicle Pete returned. He more or less surrendered himself into custody because a pack of tawny North American birds had set upon him, I guess because he put on airs.

And so it was that, on a warm summer night a week or so later, Vince told us the whole story of Pete's escape. There was a raspberry light in the western sky and cold beer at hand. The newly reclipped Pete was perched on Vince's shoulder.

We all had a good laugh, including Popsicle Pete, who (it turned out) was preparing to have the best laugh of all. Because moments later, Popsicle Pete lifted off from Vince's shoulder and wobbled like Icarus through the evening sky.

He caught a thermal, banked left toward some woods several hundred yards away, and came to rest high up in an enormous tree.

There was a moment of stunned silence.

Vince hurried down to the woods and entreated Popsicle Pete to return. And then—in one of the most poignant scenes I have witnessed in my animal- and people-watching life—Vince began to whistle, as twilight fell, a tender, dulcet version of Popsicle Pete's alleged favorite song, Mr. Acker Bilk's "Strangers on the Shore."

We all watched in rapt fascination. So did Popsicle Pete. I think the difficulty was that, as much as he enjoyed the serenade, he could hear it just fine, thank you, in the tree.

After quite a bit of whistling, Vince abruptly lost his composure, gesticulated sharply at the bird, and, in his best Queens, called Pete a compound word which, in bird circles, would have sort of a double meaning. "Awright, die up there," he hollered, and stalked back up the hill to his house to call the cherry-picker guy and to be glowered at by his aged father.

Then he stalked back down the hill to plead some more with Popsicle Pete. This time, he got results, sort of. The parrot flew down out of the tree, circled for a landing, and then pulled out of his dive, heading back up to another tree. Those of us present agreed that Popsicle Pete, who had not made a whole lot of landings in his life anyway and who was missing quite a few aerodynamically critical components, did not feel he could slow himself down enough to drift to a comfortable stop.

As the only animal expert present on the scene, I helpfully suggested that we buy some shaving cream and, as they do for disabled aircraft, create a blanket of foam on the runway. I encountered disapproval.

Twilight deepened into night. It was impossible to see Popsicle Pete, much less save him. The mood at Parrot Control (the living room) grew somber as a wake. We went home.

The following day, we got word of Pete's rescue. I have never succeeded in piecing the scenario together, because Vince and Annie grow shrill when it is discussed. I do know that it involved several changes of perch by the parrot and that, at one point, Vince, who is an expert marksman in addition to his other attributes, fetched a handgun and, I kid you not, shot off the branch Popsicle Pete then occupied.

As of this writing, Popsicle Pete is home, and normality—insofar as there can be normality in a household containing all of these presences plus a few more which I lack the energy to describe here —reigns in the house.

What's more, I believe Vince has established himself, in Pete's eyes, as a person to be reckoned with. And a damn fine whistler. Which counts for something, among birds.

I Remember Llama:
A Letter from Maine

Dear Dave,

A restaurant up here in Maine advertises dinner served with "the cocktail of your choice."

A fine idea, that. I am at the end of my tether with those restaurants where they bring you any old cocktail which they have arbitrarily selected for you. Some of them are quite nasty.

Maine is an odd place. We have come up here to be with llamas, which is odd enough.

We drove up to the Telemark Inn and Llama Farm on a bright, warm September day in southwestern Maine. The inn is a pleasant but nondescript white farmhouse sitting on some land near the Sunday River, just outside Bethel.

Before we could unload our bags and check in, an Old English Sheepdog sprang off the porch and attempted to get in our car. A pleasant-looking young man came forward, trailed uncertainly by a small, furry black goat.

"You're here," the young man said. "First thing we have to do is catch one of the llamas. Think you could help me?"

I had the unsettling feeling that he had mistaken me for someone else, but I was also seized by that curious muteness which overtakes me in unfamiliar surroundings. I nodded agreeably, and

I walked over to the corral, still trailed uncertainly and at a distance by the small black goat.

"That's William. He's not supposed to be loose," the young man said, a little vaguely.

There were seven or eight llamas loitering around the corral. As we stepped through the gate, a large, fierce-looking one hustled over and glowered at me. Most of his llama brethren were splotched with chocolate and white, but this one was a solid camel color. If I had known then what I know now about him, I would not have allowed myself to suggest, even in silent thought, that camels represented in any way a standard to which llamas should or could be held. Mocha—for that was the creature's name—would have felt strongly that camels should be evaluated strictly in terms of their resemblance, however inadequate, to llamas.

Mocha blocked my path and began to probe my neck with his snout.

"Mocha's the lead llama," the young man said. "Good. He's checked you out. He knows he doesn't like you. Now we can go."

On this insufficiently reassuring note, we commenced trying to catch one of the smaller, prettier llamas, who was having none of us. Llamas are surprisingly quick when they want to be, and they want to be when they think someone wants them to do something. It took about five minutes and the help of the sheepdog to back the llama up against the fence, where we could drop a halter over him. Mocha watched the whole escapade from a vantage point roughly two inches from the back of my head, prepared to intervene if the commonly understood laws of human-llama interaction were not obeyed.

As we brought the haltered llama out of the corral, a battered van pulled up, and another man climbed out. He was powerfully built, with the hawklike face of a Norse raider. He was a take-charge person, and within minutes he had spread among everyone present, except perhaps William the uncertain goat, the understandings that

1. My wife and I were paying guests and not whomever we had been mistaken for.

2. He was Steve Crone, owner of the Telemark Inn and of the

llamas, and the other young man was his friend and occasional assistant Dexter Randall Richards, to be addressed as Randy.

3. He was sorry I had been asked to chase llamas before being allowed to check in, but

4. We had caught the wrong llama anyway.

And thus did we begin our brief lives as llama trekkers.

Steve's purpose in keeping llamas in Maine is to introduce an element of novelty into backpacking. Steve and Randy lead short expeditions into the wilderness. The llamas carry virtually all the gear, so the hiker can wander unencumbered. Well, unburdened, anyway. Each hiker is responsible for managing a llama, which can require a fairly steady level of attention.

We spent a night at the inn and set out the next morning to climb nearby Speckled Mountain. The llama season, such as it is, was in its waning days, so the expedition party consisted only of me, my wife, Steve, Randy, Brewster (the sheepdog), and four llamas: Mocha, Alphonso, Pierre, and Raphael. Two other llama fanciers had driven over from a nearby town to accompany us on part of the hike, but they turned back around lunchtime.

Because the start of the trail was about ten miles away from the inn, Steve loaded the four llamas into his van. This is a routine occurrence in his life, but for the novice onlooker it is an astonishing sight. The van does not look as though it could hold even one llama, but the animals are quite good at folding themselves up in accommodating ways. We stopped in Bethel to pick up a few odds and ends, and while the van was parked, Mocha craned his neck out the passenger window and ogled pedestrians, most of whom had either seen his act before or had cultivated—as Mainers will—the air of being unflustered by the exotic.

One exception was a blind man, who strolled over and was introduced by Steve to the llamas. There is, of course, some kind of an old saw about what a blind man knows about an elephant, depending on what part of the elephant he has touched. I forget what, precisely, it is supposed to illustrate. In any case, it was restaged, with a llama standing in for the elephant, on the streets of Bethel, Maine. And indeed, all the helpful utterances of the sighted on the scene ("It's like a horse, but its neck is like a big snake") probably served to create, in the man's mind, an image of a terrifying sort of hybrid creature that had been thought, in some pre-Columbian circles, to exist at the edge of the world.

At the start of the trail, Steve and Randy loaded up the llamas with huge panniers, and up the mountain we trudged, leading our animals with long tethers.

Llamas, in South America, are sometimes called "silent brothers," a tribute both to their usefulness as pack animals and to their insistence on being treated more or less as equals. They are sure-footed and seemingly tireless, but that is no guarantee of their total cooperation.

In no time at all, in fact, Raphael decided to sit down on the trail. There is usually a reason for a llama's recalcitrance. Sometimes, for instance, its burden has slipped into an uncomfortable position. Other times, however, the reason is something only the llama knows.

"Now," Steve said *sotto voce*, "we have to start playing llama games."

Steve is eerily aware of the psychodynamics among his llamas. When they cop an attitude with him, he frequently has his next move already planned. His idea of "llama games" includes a number of remarks which may be addressed to a llama or a simple reordering of the procession, itself a rather complex affair in which the individual likes and dislikes of each llama must be carefully weighed. At the time of our trek, for example, Alphonso had entered a phase of adolescent hero-worship for Mocha and would cry if he was not either immediately behind or ahead of his idol in the line. Raphael's work stoppage on this day was solved by the simple act of moving him to the back of the line.

My wife led Alphonso, the youngest and gentlest llama, for the entire trip. I took turns working with Raphael, Pierre, and, yes, even Mocha. The most experienced trail beast among them, Mocha was generally indifferent to his place in line and to his proximity to other llamas. He was beyond that sort of thing.

Mocha's primary concern was his dignity. He did not enjoy being touched, and he, like many other sultans, considered it an affront for anyone to meet his gaze. Randy had mentioned before the hike began that Mocha had coated his sunglasses, several days before, with a patina of llama spit.

"Why?" I asked.

"Our eyes met at the wrong time," Randy answered.

I thought, in my innocence, that he was joking.

But if the story of our hike is ever made into a film, Mocha will be played by Louis Gossett, Jr., in a reprise of his "Don't you eyeball me!" performance in *An Officer and a Gentleman*. (I don't know who will play me. I always think Jeff Bridges would be a good choice, but people tell me, in a bubble-bursting tone, that I am wrong.)

I learned about Mocha the hard way, by cutting my eyes back at him while guiding him up an incline. I was given a brief warning. Mocha flattened back his ears and began smacking his lips and flexing his cheeks in the manner of a ballplayer working at his chaw.

"Walk away! Walk away!" cackled Steve. "He won't waste his spit on you if you turn your back and walk away."

I thought that was an interesting and revealing turn of phrase. In any case, Mocha had already concluded that I was worthy of his spit, and I received a mild showering of damp vegetable matter. It was not especially loathsome, but I had a feeling that Mocha had taken my status as a first-time offender into account.

Randy and Steve confided that there have been occasions when the llama's imperious ways have grown so wearisome that they fetched bottles of water and returned Mocha's fire. However, given Mocha's range, accuracy, and the multiple stomachs from which he can fetch all manner of brackish substances, most of these fire fights have merely compounded their sense of victimization.

The only one who need obey none of Mocha's rules is Brewster, the sheepdog, who, like a fool in a Shakespeare play, is somehow beyond the reach of the king. Brewster regards llamas as having been placed on this earth for his entertainment. I watched one afternoon as he vaulted over the corral fence, raced around Mocha in a tightening circle, and nipped at the animal's knees until Mocha sank to the ground. With a puckish canine grin, Brewster mounted Mocha from behind and pretended to have his way with the llama, who sat there looking unmistakably peevish.

When we reached the summit of Speckled Mountain, I became acquainted with another of Mocha's dislikes. He shares with the Amish an aversion to having his picture taken. It seemed rather unfair of him to spit on the person holding his tether, rather than the person with the camera, but I'm sure he had his reasons.

We camped that night at the summit. Our silent brothers had made it possible to bring almost anything our hearts desired, which included such luxuries as champagne. We hiked back down the next day. I will not bore you with other details of our trek, except to tell you what I learned of the story of Steve Crone and Mocha.

I have never met a man more attentive to and respectful of animals than Steve. Once I overheard him talking to someone else about why he had bought the farmhouse in Maine after years of traveling from the Rockies to the Everglades to any other wild place he could find. I heard him say, ". . . mostly I bought it for him. I wanted him to have a home for the last part of his life, a place to die after all those years of traveling. He's buried up there on the hill now." I had thought, for a second, that he was talking about his father, but it subsequently dawned on me that he was referring to his dog.

Steve found it difficult to think about getting a new dog after that one died. His father solved the problem for him by buying him a llama at an auction. The llama had been given to some nuns, who could not manage him. A llama seems like an odd bequest to North American nuns, but my impression of nuns is that they can manage just about anything. Not Mocha. I am not sure that even the monks of New Skete would have been up to Mocha. Had he remained within the ranks of Roman Catholicism, it would have been necessary to ship Mocha to Rome for a meeting with someone whose authority and dignity might have seemed, to Mocha, almost commensurate with his own.

In any case, Peter's Church turned its collective back on Mocha, who fell instead into the hands of a lapsed college football player. Steve Crone was blissfully ignorant of llamas, which was probably good, because Mocha arrived in Bethel harboring two big secrets about himself:

1. He was part guanaco. A guanaco is a South American animal resembling a llama, but it is considerably wilder and much less revered. A Venezuelan man once came to stay at the inn, recognized Mocha for what he was and informed Steve that "guanaco," in some circles, is also an insult to be hurled at especially unpleasant persons.

2. Mocha was what is called, among llama fanciers, a "berserk male." It is thought by some that the seeds of berserkery are sown when an infant male llama is bottle-fed. He becomes confused about the distinctions between himself and humankind. When he reaches puberty and is urged, hormonally, to assert his dominance over the other members of his herd, he is as inclined to test the mettle of humans as of llamas.

Steve gradually made the acquaintance of other llama ranchers. When it became known that he owned a berserk male, the advice was always the same: Have him put down.

Steve was disinclined to go along with them. First off, he is the type of outdoorsman who feels genuine remorse when a bug jumps into his campfire skillet and dies.

Second, he had spent much of his adult life leading delinquent human teenagers into the wilderness in Outward Bound programs. He had won the respect of some very tough young people, and what he faced now was essentially a very big Dead End Kid on hooves.

Then too, Steve was a college football player. Although he now professes disillusion with that whole world, he looks as though he could step into a uniform and get a walk-on job as an NFL linebacker.

So he and Mocha settled down to spend a long, interactive winter together. Steve had decided he would train Mocha, even if he wasn't entirely sure what "train," under these circumstances, meant.

Initially, it meant survive.

Mocha's feeling was that Steve would show him a good deal more respect after he had been charged and knocked to the snowy earth repeatedly. Llamas know not of the Marquis of Queensberry. Mocha's most alarming tactic was to rear up on his back legs and snap his front hooves out at Steve, like a charwoman shaking out a rug.

In the dead of winter, Mocha took to charging out from the cover of snowbanks.

"It was like: Mocha? Mocha?" Steve imitated Inspector Clouseau creeping around his apartment in anticipation of an assault by his houseboy Cato. "I felt like a kid on his way to school, knowing the local bully would attack him soon but never knowing exactly when."

Steve responded with a kind of Tough Llove. He had to establish himself as a llama of consequence, which meant pushing Mocha into snowbanks and generally outmaneuvering him in the most humane way possible.

One morning, however, something snapped. No one likes to live in stark terror of a herbivore. Before he knew what he was doing, Steve had put on a kayaker's helmet, knee and elbow pads, and a take-no-prisoners attitude. He stepped outside. He stepped back inside. Steve had discovered that Mainers will warm up to you to the point of returning your wave after you have lived alongside them for ten years or so without committing any acts of outright depravity. By owning a llama, Steve figured he had already set himself back another five years from his first neighborly wave. Cavorting around in an outlandish llama-jousting costume could push him into the year 2000.

As a compromise, Steve discarded the helmet. He went back outside and glared at Mocha. They began their daily training session.

"Just try something, and I will kick your ass," Steve muttered.

Nothing.

"Go ahead, try something."

Nothing.

For the moment, Steve Crone owned the most docile llama in the civilized world.

Thus does life so often deprive us of a catharsis. When we have worked ourselves up into a sufficient dudgeon, when we are ready at last to switch to a scorched-earth policy, our nemesis senses the change and gives in with a big smile.

Out of such breakthroughs (we think again of Annie Sullivan) are trekking llamas gradually pieced together.

And so it is that Mocha is now the llama who teaches each of Steve's new acquisitions. And so it is also that Steve now gets the occasional call from a llama owner looking to unload a berserk male llama or some other supposedly incorrigible animal on him. Brewster, in fact, was sent to Telemark as the last alternative to a death sentence. He is now one of the best dogs I have ever seen, apart from his rather strange sexual proclivities.

We have left Bethel now, left there with a feeling of fondness for Steve and his menagerie but also with a feeling that another year might pass before we really long for the company of a llama.

We traveled across Maine and were in Bar Harbor the other day. A story on the front page of the Bar Harbor *Times:* KNIFE-WIELDING SATANIST ARRESTED. We all sleep easier.

Actually, we felt quite safe from satanists at our bed-and-breakfast place. It is run by a couple who, I gradually figured out, are devout Christians. I believe they must advertise their inn in Christian publications, because some of the other guests were like-spirited.

I became friends with a fundamentalist Christian certified public accountant who said he, in his salad days (grant unto Caesar?), had toured in a "Christian version of Up With People." Hmmm. I presume it resembled Up With People, except, of course, with much less sex and violence.

I have enjoyed the company of these devout folks, but then, you know, I also have my moments where I feel kind of sorry for the knife-wielding satanist, who, on closer inspection, cuts a figure of much less pluck and dash than his headline might suggest.

The news story revealed that he had gone alone into the woods to perform a satanic ritual which consisted of drawing a pentagram in the dirt and cutting his finger. (It's the off-season up here, you understand. I'm sure the local satanist community really pulls out all the stops in July and August.)

Three local men, thinking he looked suspicious, had followed the satanist into the woods. The suspicions of Mainers are easily aroused. The Maine version (see above) would be Up (to a Point) With People. One of the three men was named—you'll just have to take my word on this—Milo Dunphy.

The satanist discovered his watchers in the woods, and an altercation ensued. The satanist ran after Dunphy and Co., who had experienced a loss of nerve. A police spokesman said the satanist was holding his knife in a menacing manner. I feel that it is rather difficult to run after someone while holding a knife in a manner that does not appear menacing. Unless you run while holding the blade and extending the hilt, in a sort of high-speed Surrender at Appomattox.

Maine is an exciting place.

My wife and I—now llama-tested for battle—hiked up Mount Champlain the other day, just as you and I and some others did roughly twelve hundred years ago, in our college days. It was the same kind of sunny day this time up, but much windier. Or maybe I mind the wind more.

We reached the summit and crouched in the lee of a big rock. Lo, a group of college students came up the trail, rising up over the last ledge, so that I saw first head, then shoulders, torso, etc.

They capered around and entertained each other. One of them did imitations of various noxious authority figures. Even though Thona and I had never seen the originals, we shook with silent laughter in our hiding place.

Then they were gone, tramping down another trail, their voices drifting back to us on the wind. They were so familiar—ghosts of an old life pried away from us by time. I felt sad to be so much older and sad for them, because they will age just as quickly and be just as surprised. But I felt happy too. I don't know why. Happy just to have made it to wherever I was, I guess.

We have stopped here in Kennebunkport on our way home. There is a beach here full of birds who look fat and disconcerted, the more so because I have been laughing at them. When the wind strikes up suddenly, it makes them walk backward on the beach. They glance around furtively, hoping that nobody has seen this, and there I am, laughing.

Last night we were up in our room when I realized that the sun was setting, so I roused Thona from her nap and sped with her to the beach. We ran to the jetty and clambered across its rocks to the eastern tip, where the last orange light lingered for a moment. It was one of those places where, in order to take a longer drink from the sunset, you have to run away from it first.

So tonight is our last night in Maine. We will go out and drink a toast with the cocktail of our choice. Up with people: Christian CPAs, lonely satanists, college students, berserk males of various sorts. They will all work it out among themselves. Up with llamas. Up with birds too.

I learned a lot on this trip, and now I am going home to forget it all. Within days, I will doubtless come to believe that there is something, other than a sunset, worth running for at day's end.

Right now, however, I have time to lie in the cool Maine afternoon sun and think up words for the slide and spill of time across our lives, until I drift off into sleep. . .